RETURNING HOME

A SPIRITUALITY OF THE CHRISTIAN JOURNEY

REV. DENNIS BILLY, C.SS.R.

En Route Books and Media, LLC

St. Louis, MO

I0232978

⊕ *ENROUTE*
Make the time

En Route Books and Media, LLC
5705 Rhodes Avenue
St. Louis, MO 63109

Cover credit: TJ Burdick
Cover Image: Garden Path at Giverny,
1902 by Claude Monet

Library of Congress Control Number:
2020941724

ISBN-13: 978-1-952464-18-8

Dedication

To the retreatants of
Notre Dame Retreat House
Canandaigua, New York

Epigraph

You have made known to me the ways of life;
you will make me full of gladness with your
presence.

Acts 2:28

Contents

Preface

This book is the fruit of a series of retreats entitled "Our Spiritual Journey," given in 2019 as a member of the staff of Notre Dame Retreat House in Canandaigua, New York. It does not reflect everything I shared during those retreats but uses them as point of departure for further reflection. What I do is try to delve more deeply into the nature of the spiritual life and allow the metaphor of the journey to unfold in a way that touches both mind and heart.

Hovering in the background of my reflections is the notion of the Church as a pilgrim people, a gathering of believers who look to Jesus of Nazareth as their Redeemer, follow him beyond the pale of death, and journey with him for all eternity into the mystery of the divine. The early Christians were known as followers of the Way (Acts 9:2) because they followed in the footsteps of the Lord Jesus. His way was (and is) the way of the cross. To follow him is to immerse ourselves in his paschal mystery and, in doing so, become partakers of his risen life. Sharing in Jesus' passion, death, and resurrection, in other words, is what it means for us to be fully alive.

We all want fullness of life. We all hunger and thirst for righteousness. We all seek the kingdom of God. We all desire to see God face to face. We all share a common yearning for transcendence. We all yearn for heaven. We all wish to dwell in the City of God. Deep down inside, we all long for something beyond the pale of this earthly life. That is our hope and deepest desire. This book reminds us of the return journey, our journey home, our journey to the house of the Father.

I wish to express my sincere thanks to the other members of the staff at Notre Dame Retreat House—Fr. Frank Jones, C.Ss.R., Sr. Carole Proia, S.S.J., and Mrs. Nancy Lynch—for their friendship and companionship that enabled us to work as a team and, as a result, make the retreats so well-received and beneficial to so many. I also wish to thank all those who came to the retreats for their desire to grow in their own spiritual lives, to put into action what they learned, and to share it with those around them. To these brave souls, I dedicate this book.

Dennis J. Billy, C.Ss.R.

Introduction

The spiritual life has often been presented in terms of a journey. Most of us are familiar with what that entails. Be it a vacation to a nearby resort, a pilgrimage to a foreign land, or a short trip to the local store, each journey begins, gradually unfolds, and eventually draws to a close. What is more, each one also involves a certain amount of preparation. Nor would it be uncommon to encounter certain hardships (even hazards) along the way. The reason why the metaphor of a journey is applied to the spiritual life is because the latter is all about finding our way to God. For Christians, the spiritual journey has to do with following Christ into the mystery of the divine. Jesus says, "I am the way, and the truth, and the life" (Jn 14:6).[1] We follow him, because he knows the way to the Father. We walk in his

---

[1] Unless otherwise stated, all Scripture quotations come from *Holy Bible: New Revised Standard Version with Apocrypha* (New York: Oxford University Press, 1989).

footsteps because we know that our happiness is intimately related to our journey into the mystery beyond the pale of death. We were made for God. Our happiness lies in him alone.

This book is about our spiritual journey and focuses specifically on our destination. We are all homeward bound. We are all returning home. We all long to go beyond ourselves. We all yearn for transcendence. What is more, we all want to be happy. We all wish to find rest in something greater than ourselves. Whether we believe in him or not, on some level, we also all long for God. This inner thirst is very deep, very real, and sometimes even palpable.

"Heaven" is our home. In recent years, this word has been given a bad rap. Some think it is too simplistic a concept to be entertained by their sophisticated modern (or postmodern) tastes. Others see it as a relic of the past, an outdated metaphor that has long ago served its purpose and now needs to be discarded to the waste bin of history. Still others have such a stereotyped notion of what it means (angels with harps floating on clouds) that they have dismissed it out of hand, at least until something better can be put in its place. Still others see it as a distraction from our real work of building God's kingdom of peace and social justice in the here and now. Whether we embrace the word as is or are dissatisfied with it because of what it is not and wish to replace it with another, in the end, we need to recognize the limitations of human language and see that "heaven," as a word, represents nothing more than our deepest longing and that, in the Christian tradition, it refers first and foremost for our yearning for God. In the end, we all long to be with God. We are all hardwired for God. He is present in the world and, whether you believe in him or not, he is also present in *your* world. He longs to speak with you. He longs to befriend and commune with you.

This book seeks to map out some of the major contours of our spiritual journey. Chapter one, "Where It All Begins," looks upon our spiritual journey as one that begins and ends in God. Since we have been created in the image and likeness of God, we are called to reflect in our own lives the creative, redemptive, and sanctifying actions of our loving God. Chapter two, "What Must We Do?" sees Jesus as the person we must seek to emulate. We do this by entering into the world of those we serve, giving ourselves to them completely, becoming a source of nourishment for them, and being for them a source of hope. Chapter three, "Putting on Christ," focuses on the imitation of Christ as a means for allowing God's grace to take root in our hearts. We clothe ourselves with Christ so that the Spirit, already working within us, can complete his transforming task. Chapter four, "Led by the Spirit," identifies life in the Spirit the key to successful discipleship. If we are led by the Spirit's promptings, we are sure to find our way home. Chapter five, "Returning Home," affirms that we belong in the presence of God. Heaven is both the place and the state of mind whereby we see God face to face. Because God is infinite, our journey into the mystery of the divine never ends. Each of the chapters end with a series of reflection questions under the title "Returning Home," designed to help readers delve more deeply into their own personal spiritual journey, and a short, heartfelt prayer. After a brief summarizing Conclusion, the book ends with a guided meditation, "Our Spiritual Journey," about our earthly sojourn and a poem entitled, "The Traveler's Rest." The purpose of these closing reflections is to help readers enter prayerfully into a quiet reflection on their own lives and where God may be leading them in the present moment.

Our spiritual journey is one rife with many challenges, joys, and hardships. No two journeys are exactly the same. We travel together. We travel alone. Our hope is that, one day, we will have finally arrived, finding ourselves rejoicing with one another in complete and total communion around the table of the Lord.

Chapter One

Where It All Begins

Where does our spiritual journey begin? Where does it end? What happens in between? How we answer such questions will tell us a lot about our underlying assumptions about ourselves and the world around us. It will also reveal some of our basic beliefs (or lack thereof) concerning God and the way he interacts with us. As Catholics, we believe that our spiritual journey begins and ends in God. God speaks his Word, and his Word does not return in vain. Jesus Christ, God's Word or *Logos*, is "the Alpha and the Omega, the first and the last, the beginning and the end" (Rev 22:13). He both reveals and fulfills God's Providential plan for the cosmos. That plan is intimately tied up with our spiritual journey and especially with our life of prayer.

At the Summit of Our Faith

As Catholics, we profess many truths of the

faith, the most important of which are found in the Creed we profess every Sunday at the celebration of the Eucharist. Some truths of the faith, however, are more important than others. For example, even though both are true, our belief in the divinity of Jesus is more important than our belief in Mary's Immaculate Conception. Similarly, our belief in Jesus' Resurrection is more important than our belief in Mary's Assumption into heaven. There is in the Catholic faith something called the "hierarchy of truths." That is to say, we can look at the various truths of our faith and prioritize them in such a way that places the more important ones in a higher position than the others. Picture the various truths of the faith as forming a tall mountain peak. The higher up we go the more important will be the truths that we find. At the very top of the mountain, when we reach the summit, there is one truth that outshines all the rest: our belief in a Triune God—Father, Son, and Holy Spirit.

All the other truths of the Catholic faith flow from our belief in the Most Holy Trinity. This is the most fundamental truth of our belief system. Everything else pales in comparison. It is important because it tells us that Love, not Chaos, underlies all of reality. God is not some detached, impersonal force or a fickle, domineering tyrant who governs according to his slightest whims. Nor is he a being of cold-hearted, compassionless Reason or a wrathful judge who seeks to exact vengeance for our slightest misdeeds. "God is love," we are told (1Jn 4:8), and everything he does he does out of love. Through our belief in the Trinity, we affirm that Love is the primary force from which everything else flows. The downward, catabolic pull of life that leads to decay and decomposition is no match for the upward, anabolic pull that integrates lower forms of existence into higher and higher entities. Each of us will one day die and be committed to the earth and return to the dust from which we came (Gen 3:19). Because we believe that Love has brought all things into existence and sustains them in being, we assert that Love will conquer Death (indeed, already has) and will lead us to an even higher form of existence, one continuous with our present lives, but much more than anything we have yet experienced. Jesus' resurrection from the dead is but the first fruit of this upward, anabolic movement. As St. Athanasius of Alexandria (295-373) reminds us, "God became human so that humanity might become divine."[1]

What is more, to say that God is Love already points to our belief in the Trinity. Love by its very

---

[1] See Athanasius of Alexandria, *De incarnatione*, 54.3. See also Gregory of Nyssa, *De opificio hominis* 16.

nature is oriented toward some Other. If God is Love, then there must be within the very nature of the Godhead an Other for God to Love. The dogma of the Trinity states that this Other is God's Only Begotten Son, the Eternal Word of God, who has been generated from God the Father from all eternity. The dogma also affirms that this Other is just as Personal as the Father himself and that the bond between them is Personal as well. The Holy Spirit proceeds from the Father and the Son and is the glue that binds them together, making them an intimate community of Love existing from all eternity and for all ages to come. The mystery of the Trinity thus reveals to us a Personal God who, at one and the same time, is mysteriously both One and Three. He is more than personal (as we know it). He is what C. S. Lewis would refer to as Supra-Personal.[2] Our own understanding of personhood, in other words, is but a faint re-flection, of the mystery of Love that lies at the heart of all reality.

God's Three Great Acts of Love

The Holy Trinity—Father, Son, and Holy Spirit—this intimate community of Love existing from all eternity, constitutes the underlying fabric

---

[2] C. S. Lewis, *Mere Christianity* (New York: Macmillan, 1943), 140-45.

of all Reality. This divine love could hardly contain itself. By its very nature, it is self-diffusive and looks outward, beyond its own internal relations. The God of Love, in other words, was not satisfied with simply loving what was within himself. He wanted to share this love with someone and something beyond himself. For this reason, we speak of God's three great acts of love: Creation, normally associated with the Father; Redemption, normally associated with the Son; and Sanctification, normally associated with the Holy Spirit. Even though one of the Persons plays a primary role in any particular action, it is important to remember that, despite this unique allocation of parts, the Triune God always acts as One. Let us look at each of the great outpourings of divine love.

Creation. Our God is a Creator God. He brought all things into existence and keeps them in existence from one moment to the next. He did not create the universe some billions and billions of years ago simply to leave it on its own. He created it, is still creating it, and will continue to create it. Creation, we might say, is *guttatim*, a Latin word that means "drop by drop." If God stopped thinking of his creation, it would simply fall into nothingness and disappear. To be sure, it would be impossible to speak of our Christian journey if we did not have a world to journey in. This first great act of God's love was to give us a world, nay, a universe, to live in and travel through. Yet even that was not enough for him: our God was (is) also a God of variety. He did not give us merely one type of plant, or tree, or bird, or fish, or cat or dog, or planet or star, or galaxy, or universe, but many! He even gave us many kinds of people, many nationalities, many races, many cultures, many religions, and the like! Our God, in other words, did not merely create; he was also very creative!

Redemption. But there is more. The God of Love did not merely create all that exists out of love. When he saw that something went awry with his creation due to humanity's desire to rebel against God and go its own way, he decided neither to abandon the world and leave it on its own, nor to destroy it and start all over again, but to enter our world and repair it from the inside out. God's response the humanity's sinful pride— that deeply rooted desire we have to exchange places with God, put ourselves the center of the moral universe, and make ourselves the ultimate arbiters of right and wrong—was to become one of us (in the mystery of the Incarnation), give himself to us completely, to the point of dying for us (in the mystery of Jesus' Passion and Death), become nourishment for us (in the mystery of the Eucharist), and become a source of hope (in the mystery of Jesus' Resurrection). God redeemed the world by allowing his Son to become human in the person of Jesus Christ who, as the New Adam, took our sinfulness upon himself, defeated death, and created the world anew.

Sanctification. But there is still more. God did not merely enter our broken world to repair it from the inside out. He had much more in mind for the world he created and the people he loves. He decided not merely to enter our world some 2,000 years ago in the person of Jesus Christ. He wanted also to enter *your* world and *my* world. He wanted to dwell within our hearts. And that is why he sent us his Spirit: to purify and sanctify our hearts so that he could dwell within us and befriend us in a very loving and intimate way. "The paradise of God," St. Alphonsus de Liguori (1696-1787) tells us, "is the heart of man."[3] Each person created by God is unique and irreplaceable. As each facet of a diamond reflects the light of the sun in a unique way, each of us reflects the love of God in a way no one else can. By dwelling in our hearts, the Spirit divinizes us and enables us to share in the divine nature. Ironically, God's plan all along was to allow us to share in his divinity. What

---

[3] See Alphonsus de Liguori, *The Way to Converse Always and Familiarly with God* in *The Way of Salvation and Perfection*, vol. 2, The Complete Works of St. Alphonsus de Liguori, ed Eugene Grim (Brooklyn: Redemptorist Fathers, 1926), 395.

Adam and Eve tried to take for themselves when they ate of the forbidden fruit from the Tree of the Knowledge of Good and Evil, God gave freely of his own accord by spilling his blood on the Tree of Life.

Our Spiritual Journey

Questions arise. What does our belief in a Triune God of Love who creates our world, redeems us, and sanctifies us have to do with our spiritual journey? How do these beliefs affect the way we live our lives? What practical significance do they have for us in the circumstances of our daily lives? To put it quite simply: Because we are created in God's image and likeness, they have everything to do with what we need to know about ourselves and how we find our way home.

According to the creation story in the book of Genesis, "God created humankind in his image, in the image of God he created them; male and female he created them" (Gen 1:27). This verse tells us that we reflect God's image both individually and in the relationship between men and women. As individuals, the Triune God is reflected in our memory (Father), in our reason (Son), and in our will (Spirit). His image is also reflected in the love between man and wife as ratified and made sacred in the sacrament of matrimony. The presence of this double reflection of God's image in us tells us that, like God himself, we are hardwired for love. We are born for love; we live in love; we die in love. Without love in our lives we wither and fade; we turn in on ourselves and lose touch with our true identities.

Like God the Father, we are called to be creative in our walk through life. He has empowered us with the ability to create—and even procreate! What is more, think of all the works of literature, art, and music that humanity has created over the years. Think of all the things men and women have built with their hands, the buildings, the roads, the inventions, the farms and businesses! We have the ability to shape the world around us. Because of our free will, we also have the ability to disfigure it. God placed Adam and Eve the Garden of Eden and told them to be stewards of his creation. We are called to be creative people as we walk through life, because God is creative by his very nature and we are created in his image and likeness. The one difference between us is that God creates out of nothing, while we create out of the gifts God has showered upon us in his creation.

Like God the Son, we are also called to be a healing, redeeming presence for those who journey with us through life. Redemption is past, present, and future. Jesus redeemed the world some 2,000 years ago through his passion, death, and resurrection. He continues his redemptive mission today through the members of his body, the believing community. Christ is gradually drawing all things to himself. The broken world in which we were born is being healed this moment by the power of his cross and our sharing in it through our own suffering and death. Christ's passion and death, in other words, gives meaning to our own. He loves us so much that he invites us to share in the great act of love that has been entrusted to him by the Father. He invites us to share in his redemptive mission and asks us to allow him to live in our hearts so that he can heal our own wounds and those who journey with us. Jesus, the Wounded Healer, invites us to bring our wounds to him so that he can heal us and use us to be a healing salve for others. With St. Paul we are called to rejoice in our sufferings, for they are "completing what is lacking in Christ's afflictions" (Col 1:24).

Like God the Holy Spirit, we are also called to have a transforming, sanctifying influence on those we serve. God entered our world not only to heal it, but also to transform it by elevating us to heights never before imagined. He desires to lift us up so that we can rise above our brokenness, transcend our earthly limitations, and share in the divine nature itself. This process of divinization (or *theosis*) is the work of the Spirit poured himself out on Pentecost into the hearts of the faithful. The Spirit manifests himself in our lives through his many gifts and fruits. A person gifted by the Spirit possesses wisdom, understanding, counsel, knowledge, fortitude, piety, and fear of the Lord. These gifts are not abstract principles but powerful spiritual dispositions that enable us to respond to the promptings of the Spirit in our daily lives. They put us in close contact with the Spirit and enable us to follow his lead spontaneously. The presence of the Spirit in our lives also bears much fruit: love, joy, peace, patience, kindness, generosity, faithfulness, gentleness, and self-control (Gal 5:22-23). Jesus once said that you can judge a tree by its fruits (Lk 6:43-45). When God created us, we were told to be fruitful and to multiply. This refers not merely to child-bearing, but to the type of persons we are called to be. Jesus also once said that he came to light a fire on the earth. That fire is the flame of the Spirit burning in the hearts and minds of his followers. The transformation of the world will come about through such as these.

Our Inner Struggle

Of course, it is not all quite that simple. Most of us experience in our lives an inner struggle between the ways of the Spirit and the ways of the flesh. St. Paul outlines the main contours of this interior conflict in his letter to the Galatians: "Live by the Spirit, I say, and do not gratify the desire of the flesh. For what the flesh desires is opposed to the Spirit, and what the Spirit desires is opposed to the flesh; for these are opposed to each other, to prevent you from doing what you want. But if you are led by the Spirit, you are not subject to the law" (Gal 5:16-18).

In contrast to the fruits of the Spirit enumerated above, he lists the contrary works of the flesh that enslave us to sin and the darkness of the Evil One: "Now the works of the flesh are obvious: immorality, impurity, licentiousness, idolatry, sorcery, enmities, strife, jealousy, anger, quarrels, dissensions, factions, envy, drunkenness, carousing, and things like these. I am warning you, as I warned you before: those who do such things will not inherit the kingdom of God" (Gal 5: 19-21). The difference between those who follow the law of the flesh and those who follow the law of the Spirit is quite clear. The former become slaves to their unruly passions and animal instincts, while the latter have crucified their passions so that they can be transformed and incorporated into the gentle rule of the Spirit's reign. They are free because they have been transformed by grace to live as adopted sons and daughters of God. The former are possessed by their passions and the enticements of the Evil One, while the latter are filled with the Spirit and empowered to respond spontaneously and freely to its holy promptings.

Elsewhere, Paul talks about the spiritual combat that every follower of Christ must wage against the powers of darkness vying for the domination of his or her soul: "Finally, be strong in the Lord and in the strength of his power. Put on the whole armor of God, so that you may be able to stand against the wiles of the devil. For our struggle is not against enemies of blood and flesh, but against the rulers, against the authorities, against the cosmic powers of this present darkness, against the spiritual forces of evil in the heavenly places. Therefore, take up the whole armor of God, so that you may be able to withstand on that evil day, and having done everything, to stand firm" (Eph 6:10-13). The only way we will be able to hold our ground in this spiritual combat is through constant prayer. As St. Paul reminds us: Pray in the Spirit at all times in every prayer and supplication" (Eph 6:18).

Praying Always

A suitable starting point for the discussion of the various levels of prayer and their possible relation to our internal spiritual conflict is the apostle Paul's tripartite division of the human person into spirit, soul, and body (1Th 5:23). As one of the earliest anthropologies of the New Testament, it provides an important unifying principle for a proper understanding of his exhortation for us to "pray without ceasing" (1Th 5:17).

"Spirit" (*pneuma*), for Paul, stands for the innermost depths of the human person as it is open to the divine presence and awake to the God's Spirit. It is that part of the person which communes with God beneath the sphere of human consciousness and cries out, "Abba! Father!" from the depths of the human heart (Rom 8:15). In the Christian tradition, this is the level of human existence that yearns for the direct experience of God in contemplative prayer. It is that part of the human person that seeks to pierce through the theologian's conceptual constructs of the nature of the Godhead and to encounter the ultimate ground of reality as it is. Since life "in the Spirit" represents the ultimate goal of human existence, one finds here the important role in the life of the Church of mystical theology, that is, theological reflection on the nature of the human experience of the divine.

"Soul" (*psyche*), for Paul, refers to the conscious, deliberative, psychological level of human existence. Here, reason, will, and the affections play active roles in constructing the concepts upon which a positive theology of God is based. This is the level of human existence that speaks to God through the images of mental prayer. Heartfelt expressions of love, the examination of conscience, resolutions to action, prayers of petition, the meditative reading of Scripture, all find a place on this important constituent aspect of the human person. Here, rests the appropriate place for the classical understanding of theology as a science that proceeds not from self-evident principles, but from the principles of divinely revealed truths. On this level, prayer supports the pursuit of theological knowledge, but does not participate explicitly in its ongoing rational explication.

"Body" (*soma*), for Paul, refers to corporeal human existence, not in any denigrated sense (as when he contrasts "spirit" [*pneuma*] with "flesh" [*sarx*]), but as a neutral, albeit essential, element of human existence. It is that part of the person which, although under the sway of "law of the flesh" (*sarx*), has been, is, and will be redeemed by those living according in the Spirit of Christ. Prayer seeks expression even on this, the most visible and concrete of all levels of human existence: through vocal expression (e.g., singing, verbal meditations), symbols (e.g. the sign of the cross, uplifted arms, the holding of hands) and posture (e.g., kneeling, standing, bowing one's head), and the rigors of corporeal sacrifice (e.g., fast and abstinence). A theology of prayer which overlooks, disdains, or overly spiritualizes this very important aspect of human existence, must beware of the charge of Cartesian minimalism, which reduces the body to the level of a mere machine and identifies the human person with its inside inhabiting "ghost."

As developed above, Paul's anthropology and its implications for the relationship among the various forms of prayer should also be considered in conjunction with his understanding of the Church as "The Body of Christ" (Eph 1:23; Col 1:18). Borrowed in part, from the Platonic parallel of the human soul as "writ large" in the fabric of human society, the tripartite Pauline division translates into the Spirit, Christ as the head of the Church, and the faithful who form the members of his Body. Here, the social dimension of the Pauline anthropology comes to the fore, doing so in a way which highlights the fundamental communal orientation of each level of human existence. That is to say that, the contemplative, mental, and physical levels of human prayer reach their fullest expression only to the extent that they are done "in Christ" and, hence, in solidarity with all those who, in varying degrees, are incorporated into his Body, the Church. Indeed, the fullest expression of the human person at prayer is that of the community of the Church gathered around the table of the Lord. The contemplative, mental, corporeal, and social aspects of human existence come together at the precise moment when the Church and its members are most fully themselves in the presence of their God.

The point being made in the above analysis is that all of the various levels of prayer in the Church's tradition are *necessary* for human existence. Contemplation is not to be pitted against mental prayer; nor the latter against fast and abstinence, or against liturgical prayer. Because the human person is a complex, multidimensional reality, all of these forms are necessary to orient a particular aspect of the human person toward the transcendent ground of his or her being. That is not to say that a person may not be more disposed to one form than another, but only that all four levels—the spiritual, the mental, the corporeal, and the social—are necessary if he or she wishes to orient the entire self towards God. And because this process takes place within the lived experience of Christian community, each of these forms has a special role to play in the Church's liturgical prayer. This explains the importance of singing, concrete symbols, gesture, silence, imagery, and preaching in the Church's communal celebrations. From this perspective, the key question in the discussion of the various forms of prayer and what it means to pray without ceasing is not, "Which one level is appropriate for me at this moment in my own spiritual growth?" but "What is the proper balance to strike among all four both within myself and within the community to which I belong?" The question, in other words, has moved from the area of personal choice to that of the proper dynamics of personal and communal prayer. We pray without ceasing by establishing a rhythm in our lives (proper to ourselves alone) by which we are able to orient every dimension of our human makeup to the divine.

Conclusion

The Blessed Trinity may stand at the summit of the Catholic hierarchy of truths, but humanity exists as the apple of God's eye—and always will! Like him, we are hardwired for love. Our deepest yearning is to love and be loved by others. For this reason, we are called to be a creative, healing, and transforming presence in the lives of those we travel with. We are called to walk in the Spirit, be led by the Spirit, and display his myriad gifts and fruits. The best way, indeed, the only way to accomplish this is by lifting our hearts and minds to God in prayer.

Only through prayer will we be able to overcome the allures of the flesh and the many temptations that are sure to come our way. As St. Alphonsus de Liguori reminds us: "If you pray, you will be saved. If you don't pray you will be damned."[4] That is to say, if you pray, you will one day find your way to God and experience the fullness of life. If you don't pray, you will spend eternity wandering about aimlessly, trying to fill a giant hole in your soul that in the end can only be filled by God. The choice is ours to make.

Our spiritual journey may begin and end in God, but prayer is the air we breathe along the way. As St. Alphonsus reminds us, "Prayer is the great means of salvation."[5] What is more, "Everyone receives sufficient grace to pray."[6] Just as we are constantly breathing during our earthly sojourn, so must we be constantly praying during our spiritual one. We pray without ceasing by orienting every dimension of our human make-up—the physical, psychological, spiritual, and social— to God in a daily rhythm unique to each of us personally and that cannot be replicated by anyone else. In the end, we pray by allowing the

---

[4] Aphonsus de Liguori, *Prayer, The Great Means of Obtaining Salvation and All the Graces Which We Desire of God* in *The Complete Works of St. Alphonsus de Liguori*, vol. 3, *The Great Means of Salvation and Perfection* (Brooklyn: Redemptorist Fathers, 1927), 49.

[5] Ibid., 13.

[6] Ibid., 145.

Lord's Spirit to dwell within our hearts and by allowing him to commune with our spirits and cry out with us "Abba! Father!" (Rom 8:15). We are hardwired for love, because we are hardwired for God. We are all homeward bound, and heaven is our home. We come from God and one day will return to him. We are God's children, and he wants us to go to him, talk to him, and commune with him.

Returning Home

- God's love is creative. How do you reflect God's creative love in your life? Is it present in your family life? In your friendships? In your involvement in the community? In your work? In your interests? What can you do to be a more loving and creative person?

- God's love is redemptive. How do you reflect God's healing, redemptive love in your life? Do you reach out to those who have hurt you? Do you try to forgive them? Or do you hold grudges and try to get even? What can you do to bring healing and forgiveness to those around you?

- God's love sanctifies. How do you reflect God's transforming, sanctifying presence in your life? Have you experienced the Spirit's transforming power in your life?

Have you experienced it in others? What does it mean to respond to the promptings of the Spirit?

- Prayer is the spiritual equivalent to breathing. Do you consider yourself a person of prayer? What is your favorite way of praying? What is your least favorite way? When at prayer, do you engage every aspect of your human makeup: the physical, emotional, intellectual, spiritual, and communal?

- We are all on a journey. Where is the Lord calling you at this moment of your spiritual journey? How is he challenging you? How is he asking you to grow? Do you know what it is? If so, have you asked him for help? Have you asked him to travel with you as you make your way?

Prayer

Dear Lord, thank you for your love, the love that created me, redeemed me, and sanctifies me. Thank you for the gift of life and for the fullness of life you are calling me to. Help me to reflect your love in my life to those I meet along the way. Walk with me, Lord. Let me never be separated from you. Help me to turn my entire life over to you so that you might live in me and I in you. Thank you for your friendship, Lord. Let me never take it for granted. Help me to turn to you at all times, in all places, and in all circumstances.

Chapter Two

What Must We Do?

Prayer is as essential to our spiritual journey as breathing is to life. Just as it would be impossible for us to go through life on a single breath, so too it would be impossible to find our way to God with a single prayer. Like breathing, we must be constantly taking in the precious air of God's bountiful grace, allow it to nourish our souls, and exhale all of our needs. The Apostle Paul himself reminds us, "Rejoice always, *pray without ceasing*, give thanks in all circumstances; for this is the will of God in Christ Jesus for you" (1Th 5:16-18). Prayer should be so much a part of our spiritual lives that, like breathing, it should recede to the background of our awareness and allow us to go about the tasks of daily life. Prayer is not the end of the spiritual life, but a necessary prerequisite that allows it to unfold.

But what might those daily tasks of our spiritual journey be? We know *who* we are—adopted sons and daughters of God created in his image and likeness—but *how* are we to act? What must we do? As Catholics, we do not merely look to Jesus *for* the answer. He, in point of fact, *is* the answer.

The Imitation of Christ

Other than the Bible, one of the most popular and best-selling books of all time is *The Imitation of Christ*, an early fifteenth-century treatise on the spiritual life, one of the greatest expressions of the *Devotio moderna,* and an expression of late-medieval spirituality which emphasized a spirituality of heart as a reaction against the over-intellectualizing tendencies of late-medieval scholasticism.[1] Likely written by Thomas à Kempis (c. 1379-1471), a member of the Brothers of the Common Life, this treatise reflects upon St. Paul's exhortation in his First Letter to the Corinthians, "Be imitators of me, as I am of Christ" (1Cor 11:1) and asserts that growth in the spiritual life occurs by modeling one's life on that of Christ. Such imitation is not a mere outward mimicking of Jesus' actions, but an adoption of the values of the kingdom as expressed in his Sermon on the Mount, and especially in the open-

---

[1] See Thomas à Kempis, *The Imitation of Christ*, trans. William C. Creasy, commentary by Dennis Billy (Notre Dame, IN: Christian Classics, 2005).

ing lines of that sermon, the deeply profound, poetic sayings of the beatitudes (Mt 5:3-12). It emphasizes the importance of a person's close identification with Christ, one that stems from a deep, personal friendship and that culminates in a mutual indwelling of hearts so that one can say with St. Paul, "I have been crucified with Christ, and it is no longer I who live, but it is Christ who lives in me" (Gal 2:19-20).

The imitation of Christ is a theme with deep roots in the history of Christianity: St. Paul wrote about it; Thomas à Kempis made it the heart and soul of his spiritual outlook; just a few years ago people were walking around with rubber bracelets on their wrists with the letters WWJD, an abbreviation for the phrase, "What Would Jesus Do?[2] To imitate Christ means responding to the call of discipleship by taking up one's cross and following him. How do we imitate Christ? What would Jesus do? What do we need to do? To answer such questions we must look to the Gospel narrative that underlies the entire Christian message.

The Gospel Narrative

The underlying narrative of Christianity con-

---

[2] For more on WWJD, see https://www.allaboutfollowingjesus.org/what-would-jesus-do.htm.

sists of four related movements: The Word of God entered our world, gave of himself completely, became our nourishment, and remains to this day the source of our hope. Taken as a whole, these movements represent a single event, occurring, as it were, both in time and out of time, in one age, and in every age, down through the centuries, from now unto eternity. Taken individually, they correspond to different facets of the singular mystery of Christ himself: the first, to his incarnation; the second, to his earthly life and death; the third, to his institution of the Eucharist; the fourth, to his resurrection. A more complete presentation of the narrative would thus read: Christ came to us in his incarnation, gave of himself completely in both his living and his dying, gave us in the Eucharist the nourishment of his own body and blood, and promised us in his resurrection the life of a transformed humanity.

The broad scope of this narrative gives us a number of distinct advantages regarding our understanding of Christ. Questions about his relationship with the world, for example, can be considered alongside of and in relation to those concerning his divine and human makeup. Since Christ's divinity and humanity are involved in each of the four movements of this underlying Gospel narrative (incarnation, passion and death, eucharist, and resurrection), they can be looked at in a way that avoids fragmentation and preserves their complementary orientation and underlying theological unity.

The narrative also puts an end to the hierarchical prejudice which, at various times in the Church's history, has isolated a single aspect of Christ's salvific mission and hailed it exclusively as the Church's governing theological paradigm. The four movements, by way of contrast, share a fundamental theological equivalence that renders, for example, such statements as the primacy of the Christ's passion vis-à-vis his resurrection or incarnation functionally irrelevant.

Each of the four movements, moreover, approaches the Christological process from within the concerns of a particular theological discipline: the first encompasses the concerns of classical Christology; the second, those of ecclesiology; the third, those of sacramental theology; and the fourth, those of soteriology. Because of the ease with which it can be grasped, the narrative also provides a framework for coordinating spiritual experience with theological doctrine. The result is an increased sense of continuity in the minds of believers between the Church's theory and its spiritual praxis.

Taking a Closer Look

At this point, it might be helpful if we take a closer look at each of the four movements of this underlying Gospel narrative. Doing so will help us get a better grasp not only of the unique qualities of each, but also of how they interrelate to form a narrative whole.

He Entered Our World. The narrative's first movement is perhaps best summarized by the Logos theology of John's Gospel: "And the Word became flesh and lived among us" (Jn 1:14). Rooted in both the Wisdom tradition of the Hebrew Scriptures and the *Logos* doctrine of classical Hellenistic thought, this late first-century statement of anti-docetic intent points to a new entrance of God's Word in our world. In Jesus of Nazareth, this Word lived not by virtue of its creative power (as in the rest of creation), but by virtue of its own personal presence. The Word of God entered our world in a new and daring way: it lived among us, as one of us. The Incarnation thus represents a new creative moment in God's providential plan for humanity. God's humanization, in other words, anticipates humanity's ultimate divinization.

The classical questions of Christology, which concern the relationship between the divine and human in Christ, are nothing more than an attempt to understand more deeply the precise meaning of the Incarnation. The theological formulas used to express this relationship have changed and will continue to change with the growth in our perception of what it means to be human and of what it means to be divine. No formula will ever exhaust the full meaning of the mystery of the Incarnation, not even those of the Councils. For this reason, the Church must always leave open the possibility that a new formulation at a future time that will express the mystery more fully. The challenge for our understanding of Christ, therefore, is to state the relationship between the divine and human in Christ in such a way that it will, at one and the same time, remain faithful to past formulations, and expand our present understanding of the meaning of the Incarnation. Whether or not terms such as "nature," "hypostatic union," even "person" are used has little relevance to the project's ultimate intent. What is important from the standpoint of both tradition and the first narrative movement is that, however expressed, it be maintained that Christ entered this world fully, i.e., that he was fully God as well as fully human.

It should also be pointed out that, even in this first movement, the traditional questions of Christology, which focus on Christ's inner divine/human relationships, touch upon, and, indeed, actually presuppose, his outer relationships with the world. Christ not only became flesh, but also lived among us. It is precisely this "living among us" that enabled the Word in its incarnate state to define for us the ultimate meaning of our humanity.

He Gave Himself Completely to Us. The narrative's second movement is best summarized by Paul's famous words in Philippians: "... [he] emptied himself, taking the form of a slave" (Phil 2:7). These words from one of the earliest extant Christological hymns describe the extent of Christ's love for humanity and the divine character of his humble self-effacement. Christ's *kenosis*, his utter emptying of self, reveals to humanity the meaning of divine love and provides his followers with a fitting model of Christian service. Christ gave of himself completely: in his birth, in his ministry, in his obedient acceptance of death on a cross. It is the role of servant that characterizes the meaning of Christ and of all Christian existence. It represents Christ's fundamental posture toward the world and toward all humanity.

This theme of Christ's servanthood has important implications for the Church: Christ's humility serves as a model not just for the individual Christian but for every level of the Christian community. In one sense, Jesus spent all of his life on earth building community: his gathering of disciples, his openness to sinners, his healing of lepers and outcasts, his challenge to the religious authorities of his day, all represent an attempt to fashion a New Israel from the Old, one that would eventually extend its embrace beyond the strictures of race to all of humanity. Jesus accepted the cross because of his conviction that this act would herald in a new age for the community of Israel. He entered Jerusalem to face certain death, giving up slowly and very painfully his own, very human, will to live. Just as he, for the sake of the human community, emptied himself and took the form of a slave, so too must his Church, for the sake of Christ and the kingdom he sought to establish, empty itself in service to all of humanity. From an ecclesiological perspective, such a statement implies that, whenever the spirit of service is missing in the Church, Christ himself is missing. The Church, in other words, must let go of itself in order to find itself and the kingdom it represents.

This theme of Christ's servanthood also has important implications for the questions concerning the relationship between the divine and human in Christ. According to the hymn from Philippians, it was the Word of God who emptied himself, "being born in human likeness," and "being found in human form" (Phil 2: 7). In the relationship between the divine and human in Christ, it is thus the divinity of Christ that assumes the role of servant: The Word emptied itself of the powers of its divinity and took on the humanity of Jesus. This self-imposed divine limitation stands at the heart of the intimate (hypostatic) union between the human and divine in Christ and anticipates a comprehensible solution to those concerns about the extent of Christ's consciousness and the interplay between his divine and human knowledge.

He Became Nourishment for Us. The narrative's third movement is best summarized by the words of Christ's institution of the Eucharist. Of the various accounts, that of Paul preserves what is perhaps the earliest surviving Christian liturgical formula:

> ... the Lord Jesus on the night when he was betrayed took a loaf of bread, and when he had given thanks, he broke it and said, "This is my body that is for you. Do this in remembrance of me." In the same way he took the cup also, after supper, saying, "This cup is the new covenant in my blood. Do this, as often as you drink it, in remembrance of me." For as often as you eat this bread and drink the cup, you proclaim the Lord's death until he comes. (1 Cor 11:23-26).

In his final meal on earth Jesus performed a prophetic action whose symbolism revealed the very heart of his messianic identity. Having gathered his closest disciples around him, he offered bread and wine as the symbols of the New Covenant soon to be ratified by his blood. As such, this sacrament represents both a foreshadowing and a continuation of his sacrificial death. He has given of himself completely, to the point of dying and beyond, to the point of becoming nourishment for others. It is in this manner that Jesus offered his body and blood as food for a redeemed humanity. Whenever the Christian community celebrates the Eucharist, it remembers Christ's death and anticipates with joy his future coming. At the very center of Church's life and activity, the Eucharist extends to all of humanity and applies throughout all time the effects of Christ's passion, death, and resurrection.

This sacramental extension of Christ's selfless death on the cross emphasizes the *kenosis* which all who eat and drink worthily of the Lord's own body and blood must ultimately undergo. This process of self-effacing love highlights for all Christians the participatory nature of all Eucharistic worship: by breaking bread together, each liturgical community enters more deeply into the mystery of Christ's dying and rising. Nourished by this sacramental food, they are called, in turn, to become spiritually nourishing, life-giving food for others. To celebrate the Eucharist thus requires a commitment to share more deeply in the life of Christ and in the life of one's own believing community. As a result, each Eucharistic community will always be characterized and judged by the quality of its life of service. Perhaps it was for this very reason that, unlike the Synoptic writers, the author of John's Gospel allowed Jesus' ceremonial washing of the feet of his disciples (Jn 13:1-17) to take the place of the normal institution narrative.

Christ entered our world, gave himself to us completely, and became our very nourishment. The theme of nourishment has relevance not only for Christ's relationship to the community of believers, but also to the classical questions about Christ's nature. If the Word's posture of service toward the world necessitates a divine limitation which lies at the heart of the hypostatic union and of those questions which concern the human knowledge and consciousness of Jesus, it follows from our consideration of the Eucharist that the divinity in Christ can be understood to limit itself in a way similar to that of nourishment: it relates to humanity on humanity's terms, according to humanity's needs and capacities for growth. From this perspective, Christ's divinity rests at the center of Jesus' being, supplying his humanity with the qualities it needs to fulfill his ministry and messianic vocation. It limits itself, not by cutting itself off from Christ's humanity, but by allowing Jesus' human consciousness to become rooted in and fed by its life-giving ground.

He Is the Source of Our Hope. The narrative's fourth movement is best summarized by Paul's proclamation of Christ's resurrection in 1 Corinthians:

> For I handed on to you as of first importance what I in turn had received: that Christ died for our sins in accordance with the scriptures, and that he was buried, and that he was raised on the third day in accordance with the scriptures, and that he appeared to Cephas, then to the twelve. Then he appeared to more than five hundred brothers and sisters at one time, most of whom are still alive, though some have died. Then he appeared to James, then to all the apostles. Last of all, as to one untimely born, he appeared also to me (1 Cor 15:3-8).

For Paul, the certitude of faith rests upon the testimony of those who have actually experienced the Risen Lord. Their proclamation forms the basis of what should and should not be believed.

If the resurrection had never taken place, they would all be exposed as false witnesses and there would be little cause for hope. If Christ was not raised, then the faith of the Corinthians would be worthless (1 Cor 15:17); if their hope in Christ was limited to this life only, they would be the most pitiable of men (1 Cor 15:19).

In this passage, which is considered by many to be one of the earliest extant accounts of Christ's resurrection appearances, Paul draws an important connection between the resurrection of Christ and the resurrection of the dead: "If there is no resurrection of the dead, then Christ has not been raised, then our proclamation has been in vain and your faith has been in. vain" (1 Cor 15:13-14). This association has a great deal of salvific significance: Christ's resurrection is not an isolated event without any repercussions for humanity. It points, rather, to what we ourselves have in some way already experienced in Christ and hope one day fully to become: transformed, saved, resurrected, wholly ourselves. Without the Resurrection, there is nothing to hope for: faith is worthless; life is meaningless; Christ is dead. With the Resurrection there is everything to hope for, everything to live for, indeed, everything even to die for. The Resurrection verifies the truth of all that has gone before it, i.e., the Incarnation, the Eucharist, Christ's Passion and Death. And it is the testimony of Cephas, the Twelve, James, Paul, and all the others who have experienced the Risen Lord, which verifies and makes credible the meaning of our faith. We hope because others hope on account of what they have seen and come to believe.

During his life on earth, Jesus possessed the fullness of such hope. This awareness of his final destiny was rooted not in the Resurrection (which had not yet taken place) or in the testimony of his disciples (who would never have understood at the time), but in his singular relationship to his own divinity. The Word entered our world, gave of himself completely, became our very nourishment, and provided us with hope from the deep eschatological awareness that he found in himself. His hope, however, was of a selfless nature, concerned not for himself, but for his people, a New Israel under a New Covenant written in his blood. The very reason why we hope in the resurrection of the dead is because, even before his own resurrection, it was Jesus himself who first hoped for us.

Conclusion

The underlying Gospel narrative developed in this chapter emphasizes the relationship between Christ and the believer's imitation of him, the latter being an intrinsic, grace-filled response to the action of Christ in one's own life. In one respect, it reveals the very meaning and essence of *imitatio Christi*. Just as Christ entered our world and gave of himself completely to the point of becoming nourishment and a source of hope for us, so too are we called, both individually and as a community, to enter the various worlds of the people around us and give ourselves to them in a manner commensurate to that of Christ's sacrificial offering of self, to the point that we too become nourishment for them and a source of life-giving hope. This calling reveals to us the fundamental meaning of our Christian identity. It is accomplished, not by us alone, but by our cooperating with Christ working in us and influencing us by the movement of the Spirit in our lives. Imitation, from this perspective, is the human perception of what is for Christ the very process of our own divinization. His vocation, like our own, is concerned with our becoming other christs.

The way in which this process of divinization/imitation is realized will of course depend, to a large degree, upon the particular form of Christian life to which we are called. For married couples, the four movements of the Christological process will manifest themselves in the intimate love which husband and wife are called to share with each other and celebrate with their children. For a single person, they will reveal themselves in that person's relationship to his or her family, friends, and community. For a priest, they will show themselves in his relationship to his bishop, his fellow priests, and the people he is called to serve. For a religious, they will disclose themselves in his or her commitment both to community and to a life dedicated to the vows of chastity, poverty, and obedience. Although the manner in which this process is realized will vary according to the particular state in life embraced, the process itself will always and everywhere remain fundamentally the same: to enter another's world, to give of oneself completely until one has become for that other a source of nourishment and lasting hope.

Finally, the existence of this underlying Gospel narrative brings continuity to those culturally conditioned statements trying to express the meaning of Christ and the Christ-event. Like all narrative statements, however, it too is subject to historical change. While the four movements developed here form the basis of our understanding of the divine and human relations in Christ, his outer relationship with the world, and the spirituality of the believing community, it is nearly impossible to conceive of the theological expressions in which each of them is cast as not changing over time in almost direct proportion to the advances in our understanding of language and the nature of theological expression itself. Despite this rather sobering claim, our attempt to understand the meaning of the Christ-event continues unabated. It does so because, like the mystery it serves, it is a function of both humanity and divinity, of both time and eternity, of both language and the meaning it conveys. In the final analysis, the meaning of the Gospel narrative rests in the mystery of Christ himself. Words such as Incarnation, Passion, Eucharist, and Resurrection are not, in and of themselves, essential to the insights developed here. But the various facets of the singular mystery they seek to express most certainly are. For this reason, this underlying Gospel narrative receives its validation not from its historically-conditioned (and therefore limited) linguistic expression, which is always subject to change, but from Christ himself, who has chosen each movement not only as a part of his own identity and vocation, but also for us, as a part of our very own.

- Jesus entered our world, gave himself completely to the point of dying for us, becoming nourishment for us and a source of hope. In what way is this underlying Gospel narrative reflected in your own life?
- Jesus humbled himself to become one of us. What does it mean to enter the world of

another? Can you point to any concrete experiences in your life where you have done so? In what ways is the Lord calling you to humble yourself?

- Jesus gave himself to us completely to the point of dying for us. How difficult is it for you to put someone else's cares and concerns before your own? Have you ever done so in the past? How is the Lord calling you to do so in your present life circumstances?

- Jesus became nourishment for us. In what ways have you been a source of nourishment and refreshment for those around you? How have you encouraged them and given them strength? Can you point to specific times when someone else have been nourishment for you?

- Jesus became a source of hope for us. What would it mean for you to follow suit? Have you been a source of hope for others? If so, how? If not, how could you do so? In what other ways have you been Christ to others?

Prayer

Lord, help me to think, speak, and act as you do. Help in imitate you in such a way that I am becoming more and more like you. Help me to enter the world of those around me and whom I have been called to serve. Help me to give myself to them completely, even if it means dying for them. Help me to become a source of nourishment for them. Help me to be a source of hope for them. I know I cannot do this on my own. I need your help. Walk with me, Lord. Live in me. Show me the way.

Chapter Three

Putting on Christ

It is not enough, however, to know who we are or even what we must do. If we are honest with ourselves, we must humbly admit that we cannot do it by ourselves. We need help. Our journey to wholeness is not yet complete. We are still on the way. We may know who we are called to be (children of God), but we know that we still have a long way to go. We may know what we are called to do (imitate Christ), but we know that something is wrong with us deep down inside and that we cannot go it alone.

We are wounded, broken creatures, and it is so easy for us to lose hope. Time and again, we take careful aim yet miss the mark. We are always falling short of our dreams and aspirations. We may pretend that we are in control and can handle any situation that comes our way, but we are simply fooling ourselves. We are masters at the art of self-deception yet know deep down within that

we do not measure up. We struggle within
ourselves, and fall. We set out to conquer the
world and end up being conquered by it. We
wrestle with the perennial questions of life and
death and find ourselves on the losing end time
and time again. The questions we need to ask
ourselves are: How can we cope with the tension
between vision and reality? How do we live in the
gap between who we are and who we are called to
become? How do we return to the road when we
have taken so many wrong turns and, at times,
may even feel abandoned and lost with no place to
go and no one to turn to? There are no easy
answers to such deep, fundamental questions.
Each one of us must find our way as best we can.
No two journeys are the same.

Meeting Us Where We Are

No matter where we are on our journey, no
matter how many wrong turns we have taken, no
matter how many times we've become dis-
oriented, no matter how many times we've gotten
lost and unable to find our way home, Jesus
always meets us where we are and encourages us
to take the next small step in the right direction.
He does so through the promptings of his Spirit,
whom he has given to us to dwell within our hearts
and lead us along the way that leads from dark-

ness to light, from isolation and loneliness to community and the fullness of life.

There is a battle going on within each of us, a struggle between truth and falsehood, between light and darkness, between spirit and flesh. It is a battle over the human soul, a struggle that St. Paul writes about so eloquently in his Letter to the Romans:

> For I delight in the law of God in my inmost self, but I see in my members another law at war with the law of my mind, making me captive to the law of sin that dwells in my members. Wretched man that I am! Who will rescue me from this body of death? Thanks be to God through Jesus Christ our Lord! So then, with my mind I am a slave to the law of God, but with my flesh I am a slave to the law of sin. (Rom 7:22-25)

Paul understands that, left to himself, he is helpless before the law of sin at war with his members: "I do not understand my own actions. For I do not do what I want, but I do the very thing I hate. Now if I do what I do not want, I agree that the law is good. But, in fact, it is no longer I that do it, but sin that dwells within me" (Rom 7:15-17). He touches upon a very common human experience: we fail to live up to and follow our deepest instincts. We know what is good for us and want to do it, but we fail in doing so time and time again.

Elsewhere, Paul delineates the difference between the ways of the Spirit and the ways of the flesh:

> Now the works of the flesh are obvious: fornication, impurity, licentiousness, idolatry, sorcery, enmities, strife, jealousy, anger, quarrels, dissensions, factions, envy, drunkenness, carousing, and things like these. I am warning you, as I warned you before: those who do such things will not inherit the kingdom of God. By contrast, the fruit of the Spirit is love, joy, peace, patience, kindness, generosity, faithfulness, gentleness, and self-control. There is no law against such things. And those who belong to Christ Jesus have crucified the flesh with its passions and desires. If we live by the Spirit, let us also be guided by the Spirit. Let us not become conceited, competing against one another, envying one another. (Gal 5:19-26)

We belong to Christ when we believe in him. When we believe in him, he gives us his Spirit, to befriend us, dwell within our hearts, commune with our spirits, and cry out, "Abba! Father!"

(Rom 8:15). The Spirit of Christ "... helps us in our weakness; for we do not know how to pray as we ought, but that very Spirit intercedes with sighs too deep for words. And God, who searches the heart, knows what is the mind of the Spirit, because the Spirit intercedes for the saints according to the will of God" (Rom 8:26-27). The Spirit is an Advocate who helps us to pray as we ought. When we live in the Spirit, he leads us to believe in Jesus, affirm him as "the way, the truth, and the life" (Jn 14:6), and follow him to our journey's end. But what does this mean? How does this happen?

Putting on Christ

More than seventy-five years ago, C. S. Lewis gave us a clue about how this process of empowerment takes shape. In his book, *Mere Christianity,* a book that combines a series of talks given on BBC radio during World War II, he tells the story of a man with a hideous face who was forced to wear a mask that made him look better. The brief story (or, example, if you will) "... is about someone who had to wear a mask; a mask which made him look much nicer than he really was. He had to wear it for years. And when he took it off, he found his own face had grown to fit it. He was now really beautiful. What had begun as disguise had become a reality."[1] The basic point of this brief tale is that pretending to be someone whom we are not does not necessarily have negative, hypo-critical overtones, but can actually shape us into becoming the person we wish to become. If we act a certain way long enough, that way of acting can become so deeply ingrained in us that it becomes a sort of second nature to us. Action flows from being, but in another sense also helps to shape it.

Centuries before Lewis, St. Paul, writing about a very similar process, exhorts his readers time and again to "clothe yourselves with Christ (Gal 3:27), "clothe yourselves with the new self" (Eph 4:24; Col 3:10), and especially "clothe yourselves with love" (Col 3:14). One of the clearest expressions of this notion comes in his Letter to the Ephesians:

> Now this I affirm and insist on in the Lord: you must no longer live as the Gentiles live, in the futility of their minds. They are darkened in their understanding, alienated from the life of God because of their ignorance and hardness of heart. They have lost all sensitivity and have abandoned themselves to licentiousness, greedy to practice every kind of impurity. That is not the way you learned

---

[1] Lewis, *Mere Christianity*, 160.

Christ! For surely you have heard about him and were taught in him, as truth is in Jesus. You were taught to put away your former way of life, your old self, corrupt and deluded by its lusts, and to be renewed in the spirit of your minds, and to clothe yourselves with the new self, created according to the likeness of God in true righteousness and holiness. (Eph 4:17-24)

In this passage, Paul is clearly contrasting the life of the flesh with life in the Spirit. If we clothe ourselves with the virtues of heartfelt mercy, kindness, humility, meekness, patience, and especially love (Col. 3:12), we are well on the way to becoming what we most deeply desire: to be a true follower of the way, to think and act like Christ. Later, in the same letter, Paul uses the imagery of warfare and putting on the armor of God to convey the same basic message:

... be strong in the Lord and in the strength of his power. Put on the whole armor of God, so that you may be able to stand against the wiles of the devil. For our struggle is not against enemies of blood and flesh, but against the rulers, against the authorities, against the cosmic powers of this present darkness, against the spiritual forces of evil in the heavenly places. Therefore, take up the whole armor of God, so that you may be able to withstand on that evil day, and having done everything, to stand firm. Stand therefore, and fasten the belt of truth around your waist, and put on the breastplate of righteousness. As shoes for your feet put on whatever will make you ready to proclaim the gospel of peace. With all of these, take the shield of faith, with which you will be able to quench all the flaming arrows of the evil one. Take the helmet of salvation, and the sword of the Spirit, which is the word of God. (Eph 6:10-17)

Paul's is telling his audience that the way to become like Christ is simply by "putting him on," that is, "pretending to be like him!" The mask we wear is not unlike the one found in Lewis's brief story about the man with the disfigured face: It makes real what is only apparent. Matthew's Gospel says it best: "... for God all things are possible" (Mt 19:26). God knows us through and through. He sees our good intentions, blesses our meager attempts to think and act like Jesus, and mercifully bestows his saving grace upon us. Whenever we open our hearts to him, even the slightest way, he promises to heal our wounds, transform our disfigured souls, and allow us to share in his divine nature.

When we attempt to "put on Christ" by trying to be like him in thought, word, and deed, we reveal to God our deep desire to follow him along the road of discipleship. Even if we can imitate him only a short period of time, even if we fall and fail miserably time and time again, if we do not give in to self-pity, if we refuse to admit defeat, if we humbly admit our failings and get back on our feet and start trying again to be like him, then God's transforming grace will surely be at work in our hearts. If we continue to "put on Christ" moment by moment, day after day, year after year, the time will surely come when our inner selves will be completely conformed unto Christ, and we will no longer be pretending: the disguise will have become reality. It will no longer be necessary for us to "put on Christ" for he will be actually living within us, just as he lived in St. Paul (Gal 2:20) and in the myriad of disciples who took up their crosses daily to follow him and have now taken their rightful place in the communion of saints. Christ lives in us, because we live in Christ. We can "put on Christ" only because Christ "put us on" by becoming one of us. The mystery of God's incarnation leads to the mystery of humanity's *theosis* or divinization.

What Must I Bring?

If we come to think, feel, and act like Jesus by putting him on, pretending to be like him, and allowing the grace of the Spirit to work in our minds and hearts, a twofold question arises: (1) What is getting in the way of our doing so as we make our way to our journey's end? And (2) What must we bring with us on the way? If we wish to become like Jesus, we will have to let go of many things and hold onto many others. Knowing what to bring with us on our journey and what to leave behind is an essential aspect of our pilgrim journey. When he sent his disciples on their first missionary journey, Jesus himself instructed them to travel light:

> He ordered them to take nothing for their journey except a staff; no bread, no bag, no money in their belts; but to wear sandals and not to put on two tunics. He said to them, "Wherever you enter a house, stay there until you leave the place. If any place will not welcome you and they refuse to hear you, as you leave, shake off the dust that is on your feet as a testimony against them." (Mk 6:7-11)

One of the reasons why our spiritual journey

can seem so tiring and burdensome is because we are carrying too much baggage along the way. It is interesting to note that the Latin word for "baggage" is *impedimentum*, from which we get the English word, "impediment." The Roman army knew very well that what they brought with them could slow them down and hinder their progress as they moved about. Knowing what was essential to carry with them on their journey and leaving the rest behind was a key element of their military strategy. The same holds true for us. If we wish to reach our journey's end, we must take a good hard look at our baggage and be willing to jettison anything that might be holding us back. Just what might that be?

In his book *Traveling Light*, Max Lucado, the pastor of Oak Hills Church of Christ in San Antonio, Texas, offers an interesting commentary on Psalm 23 by highlighting the importance of letting go of the things that weigh us down and prevent us from making headway in our sojourn through life. A look at the book's chapter headings gives us a clear understanding of why so many of us are weighed down (even overwhelmed) by the baggage we carry with us. So many of us carry with us the burden of a lesser god, the burden self-reliance, the burden of discontent, the burden of weariness, the burden of worry, the burden of hopelessness, the burden of guilt, the burden of

arrogance, the burden of the grave, the burden of
grief, the burden of fear, the burden of loneliness,
the burden of shame, the burden of disappoint-
ment, the burden of envy, the burden of doubt,
and the burden of homesickness—to name but a
few.[2] If we carry such baggage with us on our
journey, no wonder we feel so tired and weighed
down! It was never meant to be this way. Jesus
himself says, "Come to me, all you that are weary
and are carrying heavy burdens, and I will give
you rest. Take my yoke upon you and learn from
me; for I am gentle and humble in heart, and you
will find rest for your souls. For my yoke is easy,
and my burden is light" (Mt 11: 28-30). Time and
again in the Gospel narratives, Jesus tells his
disciples, both before and after his resurrection
from the dead, "Do not be afraid."[3] With him at
our side, there is no need to carry this unnecessary
baggage with us as we journey through life. He
entered our world, probed the depths of human
experience, submitted his innocence to the
violence of death, and rose victoriously from the
grave precisely to free us from all that hinders us

[2] Max Lucado, *Traveling Light: Releasing the
Burdens You Were Never Meant to Bear—The
Promise of Psalm 23* (New York: MJF Books, 2013), v-
vi.

[3] See, for example, Mt 10:26-28, 14:26-27, 17:6-7,
28:4-5; Mk 5:36, 6:50; Lk 5:10, 8:50, 12:4-7, 12:32; Jn
6:20, 12:15.

from making our way to the Father.

Jesus' yoke is that of the cross. Although our spiritual journey can at times seem difficult, arduous (even dangerous and life-threatening), it is meant to be highly focused, purpose-filled, and determined to reach its goal. Jesus calls out to each of us: "If any wish to become my followers, let them deny themselves and take up their cross daily and follow me" (Lk 9:23). Jesus' yoke is easy to bear, because he does not ask us to carry it alone. He accompanies us on our journey and does so every step of the way. He goes before us to show us the way, beside us to befriend us on our journey, behind us to catch us when we fall, and within us through the indwelling of his Spirit. He wants us to rid ourselves of our useless baggage and bring with us instead the gift of the Holy Spirit and all that flows from this essential, primordial gift: the three things that last (Faith, Hope, and Love), the seven sacraments (Baptism, Eucharist, Confirmation, Penance, Marriage, Holy Orders, and the Anointing of the Sick) the gifts of the Spirit (Wisdom, Understanding, Counsel, Knowledge, Fortitude, Piety, and Fear of the Lord), the fruits of the Spirit (Love, Joy, Peace, Patience, Kindness, Generosity, Gentleness, and Self-control), and most especially food for the journey, the summit of the Christian life (Jesus' Body and

Blood shared at his Eucharistic Table).[4] These are the essential things we need for our spiritual journey. If we carry these precious gifts with us as we make our way in our spiritual sojourn, we will be sure to make our way home and enter into the presence of the Father.

The Threefold Way

Our spiritual journey is all about the following of Christ and the way of discipleship. As the verse from Matthew's Gospel cited above indicates, if we wish to follow him, we must do three things: (1) deny ourselves, (2) take up our cross daily, (3) and follow him. This threefold process of self-denial, bearing our cross, and walking in the footsteps of Jesus reflects what classical Catholic spirituality refers to as the threefold way of purgation, illumination, and union.

Denying Ourselves (Purgation). To be an authentic follower of Christ, each of us is called to deny ourselves by making Jesus the center of our moral universe, rather than ourselves. Doing so involves a process of purgation whereby our primary focus in life is not doing our own will, but

---

[4] See *Catechism of the Catholic Church*, nos. 736, 1113, 1304, 1322-1419,1812-21 (Vatican City: Libreria editrice Vaticana, 1994), 194, 289, 330, 334-56, 446-48.

the will of our heavenly Father. Each of us is called not to do it "My way" (as the song goes) but "God's way." Making this happen can be a long, harrowing process, for it requires a movement from complete separation of the two wills, to one of external conformity with God's will, to one of complete inner uniformity with it so that the two exist in close harmony and appear as one.

Taking Up Our Cross (Illumination). The cross is the symbol of Christian martyrdom par excellence and the badge of the true disciple. The word "martyr" comes from the Greek word for "witness" and refers to those who believe so deeply in the Lordship of Christ that they are willing to spill their blood and give their lives for the Truth. Jesus, we must remember, is not only the Way, but also the Truth (Jn 14:6). There are many ways of giving witness to the Truth. Not all disciples may be called to spill their blood for Christ, but all are called to give witness to him by living the moral life. In *Veritatis splendor*, his encyclical on the fundamental principles of the moral life, Pope St. John Paul II says living the moral life is a type of martyrdom, for it involves not only a denial of oneself, but also a willingness to suffer bravely the many difficulties which fidelity to the moral order can demand.[5]

Following Christ (Union). Jesus is not only the Truth, and the Way, but also the Life (Jn 14:6). To follow him does not mean that we walk behind him grudgingly as a slave would follow his master, but to follow as he followed the promptings of the Spirit in his own life to embrace the will of his Father in heaven and make it his own. Christ walks before us, beside us, behind us, and within us. He invites us to enter into the intimate relationship he shares with the Father. That relationship is the bond of the Spirit, who proceeds from the Father and Son from all eternity. Jesus invites us to share in his Spirit and, in doing so, participate in his divine life. When we follow Christ, we become one with him. This happens through Baptism, by living a life in the Spirit, and by following him on in his spiritual journey into the mystery of the Father's love.

In trying to understand the nature of this process of purgation, illumination, and union—especially when seen through Jesus' invitation to discipleship by means of self-denial, carrying one's cross, and then following him—we should not look upon it in a linear manner (as if purgation ceases when illumination begins and illumination

---

[5] John Paul, II, *Veritatis splendor* (Encyclical Letter, August 6, 1993), no. 93 (Washington, D. C.: United States Catholic Conference, 1996), 141-42

ceases when union takes place), but as each prior stage of the process being incorporated into the one following it. A good image to employ when envisioning this threefold way is that of an upward spiraling motion, whereby varying cycles of purgation, illumination, and union take place during our spiritual journey, with the cycles becoming increasingly smaller and smaller as we near our journey's end. The idea here is that we go through many cycles of purgation, illumination, and union during our earthly sojourn and that all of them will ultimately converge in a single point. Since each of our journey's is unique, the magnitude of these cycles will vary from one person to the next.[6]

Conclusion

The earliest Christians were known as those belonging to the Way" (Acts 9:2). To be followers of the Way means we are a pilgrim people with one foot in this world and another in the next. To take an image of St. Augustine (354-430), we are traveling through the City of Man, but our desti-

---

[6] For more on the threefold way, see *The New Dictionary of Catholic Spirituality*, ed. Michael Downey (Collegeville, MN: The Liturgical Press, 1993), "The Three Ways," s.v. Thomas D. McGonigle.

nation is the City of God.[7] As we make our way
from one city to the next, it is very important that
we let go of whatever burdens may be weighing us
down and keep only the essentials for the journey.
We are called to travel light.

Every journey has a beginning, middle, and
end. Faith keeps us focused on our final end. Hope
gives us a confident yearning that we will one day
arrive at our journey's end. Love helps us to take
the necessary steps in the daily circumstance of
life to get there. Guided by the Spirit and his
manifold gifts and fruits, empowered by the
virtues and the values of the kingdom, we make
our way through life with the understanding that
earth provides us with no lasting home and that,
as we make our way through life, we are nothing
but strangers in a foreign land. We are homeward
bound, but our home is not of this world (Jn
18:36). It lies beyond the pale of death in a
kingdom that is yet to come, yet in some strange
way already here.

Our spiritual journey begins and ends in God.
As St. Augustine so eloquently put it, "You have
made us for yourself, and our hearts are until they

[7] Augustine of Hippo, *The City of God*, 19.26, trans.
Henry Bettenson (New York: Penguin Books, 1972),
892.

can find peace in you."[8] The whole point of our spiritual journey is to find rest in God. Peace, St. Augustine tells us, is "the tranquility of order."[9] When we find peace, we experience order within ourselves, in our relationships with others, and in our relationship with God. When we follow the ways of the world, we find nothing but anxiety and discord within ourselves, with others, and in our relationship with God (or lack thereof). Jesus is the Prince of Peace. "Peace be with you," were some of the first words from his mouth after he emerged from the tomb (Jn 20:19). He wishes us to be at peace more than anything else. He offers us a peace the world cannot give (Jn 14:27), a peace that flows from God and returns to him—and never in vain (Is 55:11).

Returning Home

- God always meets us where we are and the helps us to take the next toward him. What struggles are you going through? Have you asked God for help with them? Have you tried to hide them from him and deal with

---

[8] Augustine of Hippo, *Confessions*, 1.1, trans. Rex Warner (New York: New American Library, 1963), 17.

[9] Augustine of Hippo, *The City of God,* 19.13 (p. 870)

them yourself? What practical steps do you
need to take to better your life?

- God wants us to travel light. What baggage
are you carrying with you on your journey?
Can you name those you find particularly
burdensome? How long have you been
carrying them? Why? What is keeping you
from letting go of them? What is keeping
you from giving all your worries and cares
to Jesus?

- Paul tells us "to put on Christ." Have you
tried to do so? If so, were you successful? If
so, for how long? What did you do after you
fell? Did you simply stop trying to think
and act like him? Or did you seek forgiveness, get back on your feet, and start again?
Why is the imitation of Christ so important
for your spiritual journey?

- Jesus said his followers must take up their
cross daily and follow him. What crosses
have you carried in life? How do these
crosses differ from baggage you need to let
go of? How did you carry these crosses?
Grudgingly? With quiet resignation? With
grit and determination? With joy? What
does it mean to conform your will to that of
your heavenly Father?

- Our spiritual journey often involves a con-
tinuing process of purgation, illumination,

and union. Where are you in your journey? Have you ever experienced moments of being purged and cleansed? Have you ever received a deeper insight into yourself and your relationship with God? Have you ever felt especially close, even one, with God? How have such moments shaped you? How have they helped you grow in your following of Christ?

Prayer

Dear Lord, thank you for meeting me where I am. Thank you for entering into my struggles with me and helping me to face them. Thank you for inviting me to let go of the baggage I am carrying and to unburden myself before the yoke of your cross. Help me to clothe myself with your Spirit and his manifold gifts and fruits. Help me to imitate you by thinking as you would think, speaking as you would speak, and acting as you would act. Lord, my hope is that I might one day be able to say with the Apostle Paul, "It is no longer I who live, but it is Christ who lives in me" (Gal 2:20).

Chapter Four

Led by the Spirit

Only after we have put on Christ will we be able to be led by the Spirit. Although God's grace has no doubt already been helping us to put on Christ, to be led by the Spirit requires an added docility to his internal and external promptings. This docility comes from the working of grace in our lives and is a reflection of God's providential plan for humanity. That plan has a pre-established order for humanity in general and for each of us as individuals. That order follows the immanent relations within the Trinity. How is this so?

The Father, Son, and Holy Spirit exist as an intimate community of love, but within a firmly established order. The Father eternally generates the Son; the Spirit, in turn, eternally proceeds from the love of the Father and the Son. God's external actions in the world, moreover, flow from his internal relations and manifest themselves in a variety of ways. Although God always acts as

one, each of his three gratuitous acts of love—
creation, redemption, sanctification—is normally
associated with one of the Persons of the Blessed
Trinity: creation with the Father, redemption with
the Son, and sanctification with the Holy Spirit.

The pattern within God's Providential plan for
humanity (indeed, for all creation) thus reflects
the pattern within his own nature. Christ's
redemption would not have been necessary if the
Father had not created the world in the first place.
Similarly, The Holy Spirit would have nothing to
sanctify, if Christ had not first redeemed us by his
passion, death and resurrection. If our spiritual
journey begins and ends in God, it is the work of
the Father to give us life and keep us in being, the
work of the Son to heal us of our wounds and bring
us back to health, and the work of the Spirit
transform us from within and help us find our way
back to God. As part of our spiritual journey, we
are all called during the time of our earthly
sojourn to follow the promptings of the Spirit.

A Sober Truth

In John's Gospel Jesus tells his disciples that
he must return to the Father so the Spirit might
descend upon them: "... it is to your advantage
that I go away, for if I do not go away, the Advocate
will not come to you; but if I go, I will send him to

you" (Jn 16:7). Pentecost cannot occur without the Ascension. Jesus must first ascend to heaven before the Holy Spirit can descend on the apostles and begin his work of sanctification. Christ's redemptive journey must end before the Spirit's transforming mission can begin.

This sober truth leads to the exhilarating experience of being filled with the Spirit, an event which itself leads to the Church's commission to spread the Good News to all the corners of the earth: "'As the Father has sent me, so I send you.' When he had said this, he breathed on them and said, 'Receive the Holy Spirit. If you forgive the sins of any, they are forgiven them; if you retain the sins of any, they are retained'" (Jn 20:21-23). Even though John's Gospel here has Jesus still on earth while imparting the Holy Spirit upon his disciples, the same sober truth holds true. As Jesus ends his earthly sojourn to return to his heavenly home, he breathes his Spirit upon his disciples as a parting gift and gives them the power to bind and loose from sin.

Although the Gospels may express it differently, they convey the same basic, underlying truth. It is the Spirit, not the earthly Jesus, who accompanies the disciples on their mission to preach the Gospel to the ends of the earth. The Church's historical sojourn is thus deeply intertwined with the sanctifying mission of the Holy

Spirit. The Spirit is the soul of the Church and continues Christ's mission on earth by using the members of his body as the primary instruments of the world's transformation. If Jesus came to make all things new (Rev 21:5), he does so by allowing his followers to partake of his Spirit and help in the shaping of the new creation. "The wind blows where it chooses," the Scriptures tell us (Jn 3:8). A wind swept over the face of the waters when God created the world (Gn 1:2); it swept through the entire house on the day of Pentecost (Acts 2:1); it sweeps through the human heart at the dawn of the new creation. As the Apostle Paul reminds us "... if anyone is in Christ, there is a new creation: everything old has passed away; see, everything has become new!" (2Cor 5:17).

Absence and Presence

The presence of the Spirit in the Church was made possible by Jesus' ascension to heaven. Once he returned to his Father in heaven, Jesus could now be present in a way never before imagined. His earthly absence allowed a new type of presence to take shape within the human heart. "The kingdom of God is among you," we are told (Lk 17:21). This verse can also be translated as,

"The kingdom of God is within you."[1] Jesus himself is the kingdom. When he walked the earth, he was among us, in our midst. When he returned to the Father and sent his Spirit, he could now dwell within our hearts. Jesus' ascension, in other words, made it possible for him to be present to us in a way that was more intimate than when he walked among us. No longer in our midst, he could now reside within our hearts.

Michael Casey, a Trappist monk from Tarrawarra Abbey in Victoria, Australia, draws out this intimate connection between Christ's absence and presence. In his book, *Toward God: The Ancient Wisdom of Western Prayer*, he writes:

> Let us return to the mystery of the Ascension. What does it mean? It means that the humanity of Jesus Christ which, during his career in Palestine, was radically restricted in terms of spatio-temporal presence now becomes universally accessible. In the paschal mystery the humanity of Jesus Christ remains, but it is a humanity no longer localized at specific points in space and time. It is a humanity now present at *all points* in the spatio-temporal

---

[1] See Luke 17: 21 in *Holy Bible: New Revised Standard Version with Apocrypha*, 82n.g.

continuum. The Ascension is not an occasion for a "good-bye;" if anything, it is a time for "welcome." It is a departure from this earthly sphere only in the sense that it involves transcending those limitations that constitute us as historical beings. By reason of the Incarnation, the Word became part of human history. In the state resulting in his Resurrection and Ascension this presence continues without restriction. The Word-become-flesh not only sits at the right hand of the Father; he continues to be with his disciples on earth. The final words attributed to Jesus in the Gospel of Matthew are precisely a promise of permanent presence: "Behold I am with you through all days until the consummation of the age" (Mt 28:20).[2]

By becoming absent in one way, Jesus makes himself present to us in an even deeper, more intimate way. The facets of Jesus' paschal mystery—his passion, death, resurrection, and ascension—are all intimately related and lead to a new way of being present to his people. When seen in this light, the descent of the Holy Spirit at

---

[2] Michael Casey, *Toward God: The Ancient Wisdom of Western Prayer* (Triumph Books: Liguori, MO, 1995), 162-63.

Pentecost is the culmination of God's creative, redemptive, and sanctifying action in the world, and especially within the human heart. "Paradise for God," we have been told, "is the heart of man."[3] God created this world, redeemed it, and sanctified it, so that he could live in our hearts and so that we could live in his.

God always acts as one and wishes to draw all things to himself. We were created, redeemed, and sanctified so that we could share in his divine nature. The gift of the Spirit allows us to participate in the life of the Trinity in a very close and intimate way. This gift is freely given and must be freely accepted. Unlike the Evil One, who seeks to overpower us and take possession of our souls in a violent, controlling manner, God will never seek to impose his will. He wants us to receive his Spirit openly and freely. For this to happen, however, we must open our hearts to him so that he can open his heart to us. Throughout history, God has chosen to dwell in a variety of places—in the Ark of the Covenant, in the Jewish temple, in the tabernacles of our churches—but he especially wishes to dwell within the tabernacle of our hearts. He wants us to be temples of his Holy Spirit. Our hearts, in other words, are meant to be a resting place for the Spirit so that we ourselves can find respite from the turbulent world around

[3] See above Chapter 1, note 3.

us, discover our true identity, and be led by him to our journey's end.

Spiritual Childhood

Jesus is the Son of God, and because of him we too can be called children of God. Although at baptism, we become God's adopted sons and daughters, we still need to choose what kind of children we will be. We can be like the prodigal son, who demands his share of his father's inheritance and wastes it on loose living. We can be like the elder son, who adopts a pharisaical attitude towards others and fails to appreciate the father's love for him.[4] Or we can be faithful, loyal children who accept God's deep unconditional love for us and treat him for who he is: a kind, loving, and merciful father. The choice is ours alone to make. What we are destined to become depends on this fundamental choice: to follow the way of the Lord Jesus or another path of our choosing. The way of the Lord Jesus is one of spiritual childhood. As Jesus himself attests, "Truly I tell you, unless you change and become like children, you will never enter the kingdom of heaven" (Mt 18:3).

Dom Eugene Boyle, O.C.S.O. identifies three important virtues of spiritual childhood: humility

---

[4] See Luke 15: 11-32

of heart, poverty of spirit, and unbounded confidence.[5] With regard to humility, he cites St. Thérèse of Lisieux, who says: "To be little means not attributing to self the virtues one practices, believing oneself incapable of anything; it means recognizing that the good God places this treasure of virtue in the hand of a little child to be used by him when he has need of it; but always it is God's treasure. In fine, it means not being discouraged by our faults, for children fall often, but are too small to do themselves much harm."[6] A person who is humble of heart recognizes that everything comes from the hand of God. With respect to poverty of spirit, Boylan writes, "Often we forced to admit our insufficiency. Our incapacity and our futility are only too obvious. But even then, we only admit the truth to resent it. This is where we fail. True humility, true poverty of spirit, true love of our Lord rejoices in its poverty and exults in such complete dependence on God. Grace will come to such a soul in abundance when it is needed—but there must be no piling up of reserves, no proprietorship. One has to wait for each day and each deed for the necessary help to arrive."[7] A person who is poor in spirit depends on

---

[5] Eugene Boylan, *The Priest's Way to God* (London: Catholic Way Publishing, 2014), 114.

[6] Ibid.

[7] Ibid., 115.

God for all things and in all circumstances. True confidence, Boylan maintains, comes not from "an illusory sense of our own merits," but from "the goodness of God, who is sufficiently good to overlook our lack of merit, and to be infinitely merciful to our poverty and nothingness."[8] We have confidence in God because we believe he has our best interest in mind and is looking out for us at all times. Each of these important virtues—humility of heart, poverty of spirit, and confidence in God—are intimately related. The humble person is one who is in touch with his or her deep inner poverty and utter dependence on God and who, as a result, has great confidence in God's unconditional love and mercy in every circumstance.

Children at Play

One thing that children love to do is play. Through it, they exercise their imagination, make friends, adapt to the world around them, get in touch with their dreams, and learn to reach out for them. If what Jesus says is true—that we must become like little children if we wish to enter the kingdom of heaven—then we must learn what it means to play. If we are to become like little children, we must learn how to be alone and

---

[8] Ibid.

entertain ourselves, discover how to interact and play with others, and know how to relate in playful manner with God. Children like to play with their friends. God's deepest desire is to befriend us. After all, Jesus himself once remarked, "I do not call you servants any longer, because the servant does not know what the master is doing, but I have called you friends." (Jn 15:15). Hans Urs von Balthasar called Jesus the "Eternal Child of the Father."[9] Jesus loves his Father, and he loves us. He wants to play with his friends.

Basing himself largely on Aristotle's *Nicomachean Ethics,* Thomas Aquinas (1224/25-1274) identifies three marks of authentic friendship: benevolence, reciprocity, and mutual indwelling.[10] We must wish our friends well and actively pursue their well-being; the relationship must be mutual; and we must carry each other in each other's hearts. He goes on to call charity "a certain kind of friendship with God" and indicates that friendship with God is the entire goal of the

---

[9] Hans Urs von Balthasar, *A Theological Anthropology* (New York: Sheed and Ward, 1967), 257.

[10] Thomas Aquinas, *Summa theologiae*, I-II, 26, a. 4, resp; q. 23, a. 1, resp; *Summa contra Gentiles*, III, chap. 19. See also, Paul J. Wadell, *Friendship and the Moral Life* (Notre Dame, IN: University of Notre Dame Press, 1989), 130-41.

spiritual life.[11] Alphonsus de Liguori, we have already seen, says that heaven for God is to dwell in the human heart.[12] The indwelling of the Holy Spirit is God's way of befriending us. He was not content with entering our world in the mystery of the Incarnation; he also wanted to enter our own private worlds and saw that the only way he could do that was by a mutual sharing of hearts. With the Christ's Spirit dwelling in our hearts and our spirits living in his, we are able to enter into an intimate friendship with God and partake in the divine nature. God became human, we have seen, so that humanity might become divine.[13]

God descended into our world in order to lift us up into his so that we could partake in the divine play. Because of the Spirit, we can exper-ience this intimate experience of divine love even today. An apt metaphor for this experience is that of the dance. The Spirit dwells within us and, through his manifold promptings, leads us more and more into the mystery of the divine. The Spirit wishes to sweep us off our feet, dance with our souls, and lead us into the mystery beyond this earthly realm. For this to happen, however, we must be open to his promptings and be able to

---

[11] Thomas Aquinas, *Summa theologiae*, I-II, q. 65, a. 5, resp.

[12] See above Chapter 1, note 3.

[13] See above Chapter 1, note 1.

respond to them spontaneously. When couples join in a slow dance, they hold each other close, and move as one. One follows the lead of the other, and they are able to transform the music they hear into a visible display of beauty. The same can be said for our dance with the Spirit. By following his lead, we are able to sense his promptings and follow them. We are no longer merely "putting on" Christ for Spirit is within us and showing us how to live and move and have our being rooted in the mystery of divine love.

Friends of God

In the early Church the saints were often referred to as the "friends of God."[14] They were men and women who had learned how to open their hearts to the Spirit, respond to his promptings, and enter into a dance of abandonment to the will of God. They danced in a way that was peculiarly their own. Some were missionaries. Others were teachers. Others cared for the poor and hungry. Still others comforted the sick and sought to make them well. Some established religious orders. Some were called to serve in the public sphere. Others married and had families.

---

[14] See Peter Brown, *The Making of Late Antiquity* (Cambridge, MA: Harvard University Press, 1978), 54-80.

Some were asked to make the ultimate sacrifice and give up their lives for the faith.

No two saints are alike. They appear throughout history and are more numerous than we may think. They live in time and space but have their gaze fixed on eternity. They live not for themselves, but for God and neighbor. What unites them is not what they did, but why they did what they did it. They are known as the "friends of God," because they love God and are willing to do whatever he asks of them. They each carry a cross, normally not one of their own choosing. They find meaning in the suffering it brings, for they see Christ living out his paschal mystery in them. They follow Jesus because they know he loves them, and they want to love him in return. They believe that he will show them the way to the Father and that the crosses they have been asked to bear will make them holy. Holiness, for them, is what it is all about. There is a universal call to holiness. God wants us all to be saved. He wants us all to be his friends. He wants us all to be saints.[15]

Of all the saints who ever lived, Mary of Nazareth, the mother of Jesus, was the one closest to him. She was his first— and best— friend. She was God's "favored one" (Lk 1:28), the woman

---

[15] See Second Vatican Council, *Lumen gentium*, nos. 39-42.

whom, Catholics believe, the angel Gabriel hailed as "full of grace." She was the woman who conceived by the Holy Spirit: first in her heart, and then in her womb. She brought her Son into the world and watched him die on the cross. She was the mother of sorrows, whose heart was pierced with a sword. She was also a woman of great joy, whose soul magnified the Lord (Lk 1:46). She experienced her Son in his glorified state and, having been assumed bodily into heaven, she alone, of all the human race, now experiences the fullness of redemption. For this reason, she is "our life, our sweetness, and our hope." Litanies have been written in her honor. Hymns sung to praise her pivotal role in salvation history. More than anyone else, she knew how to follow the promptings of the Spirit. She invites each of us to join in the dance. It doesn't matter if we do not know how. If we ask her, she will teach us. Better yet, she will ask her Son to show us the way. His Spirit—the Paraclete, the Advocate, the Comforter— will teach us everything we need to know. All we need to do is follow his lead.

Conclusion

Once we have allowed the light of God to cast out the darkness of sin from our hearts, once we have put on Christ and opened ourselves up to the gentle promptings of his Spirit, once we have joined in the dance of the friends of God and found our rightful place in the communion of saints, then we will have discovered our true identities as sons and daughters of God. Jesus is the Prince of Peace; as his adopted brothers and sisters, we share all in his noble heritage. Our Father in heaven looks upon us as he looks upon his Son—as one of his own.

With Jesus' Spirit dwelling within us, we share in the freedom of the sons and daughters of God. That freedom encourages us to become our truest, deepest selves and always moves us to seek out and embrace all that is One, True, Good, and Beautiful. It is a freedom bought for us by the blood of the Lamb, one that is rooted in and destined for love. This freedom in the Spirit enables us to affirm with the Apostle Paul that there are three things that last—faith, hope, and love— and the greatest of these is love (1Cor 13:13).

To be led by the Spirit is to be led by the Spirit of Love. "God is love," we are told (1Jn 4:8). The Spirit is the bond of love between the Father and the Son. God wants us to share in his divine love in as intimate a way possible. The kingdom of God is filled with the friends of God. Jesus' Spirit builds it little by little, one friendship at a time. He is in no rush. He has all eternity to wait for his wayward prodigals to return. That is not to say that he does not actively seek us out. He is the hound of heaven. He is always searching for his lost sheep. He is tireless and unrelenting in his quest to draw all people to himself (Jn 12:32). He allows those led by his Spirit to find their way home and share in that noble quest.

Returning Home

- Christ ascended so that the Spirit could descend. In what sense does the Spirit's presence require the absence of the earthly Jesus? How did his ascension to heaven pave the way for the descent of his Spirit? How is the Spirit's presence a result of the glorified body of the Risen Christ?
- "The wind blows where it chooses" (Jn 3:8). What does it mean to be led by the Spirit? Have you been led by him? If so, how did you know he was leading you? Have you ever felt as though you knew where the Spirit was leading but you chose not to follow him? How do know when it is the Spirit who is prompting you and not yourself or, worse yet, the spirit of the Evil One?
- "Let the little children come to me" (Mt 19:14). Do you consider yourself a child of

God? If so, do you manifest in your life the qualities of spiritual childhood: humility of heart, poverty of spirit, and unbounding confidence? In which of these areas do you need to grow?

- The early saints were known as the "friends of God." Do you consider yourself a friend of God? Does your life manifest the various marks of friendship: benevolence, reciprocity, and mutual indwelling? Do you relate to him as a friend? Does God consider you one of his friends?

- What does being "led by the Spirit" tell us about the pursuit of holiness? Can we achieve holiness on our own? Is it something we can earn? If holiness is a gift, why do so many people reject it? How have you responded to the Spirit's promptings in your life? In what ways have you rejected them?

Prayer

Lord, I thank you for the gift of your Spirit. Help me to be open to him at all times and able to respond to his promptings. Help me to grow in your friendship so that you might dwell in me and I in you. Bless me with the gift of spiritual childhood. Make me humble of heart, poor in spirit, and abounding in confidence in your love for me and your people. Help me to understand what it means to be a true friend of God. Help me to foster your friendship with me so that I might share the gift of your friendship with others. I love you, Lord. Help me to love you more.

Chapter Five

Returning Home

Home is where the heart is. It is where we feel welcomed, where we belong. We all long for home. It's a place where we can take off our shoes, relax, and simply be ourselves. We are constantly searching for a place where we can belong. For centuries, life in the family had given us this strong sense of belonging. It was closely knit, extended far and wide, and pointed to something beyond itself, to another, larger family—the family of God.

The situation today, however, is far different. Times have changed. Families are not what they used to be. They have fallen on difficult times, and we are reaping the grim consequences. The nuclear family of husband, wife, and children is in a state of rapid decline and will soon become the exception in Western society. The extended family, moreover, is fast becoming nothing more than a distant memory. While every family is somewhat dysfunctional (There is only one Holy Family), the degree of dysfunction has grown exponentially in recent decades, mainly because today's secular culture has lost touch with a sense of the sacred. Few families today point to something beyond themselves. They have forgotten that they are a reflection of a larger family. They have lost sight of their membership in the family of God.

Our Lost Sense of Belonging

Rather than sharing a sense of belonging, many of us today feel distant (even estranged) from our own family members. It is possible even to be an orphan in one's own home, to live in the lap of luxury but to lack the one thing we desire most: being loved by another for our own sake, regardless of what we have done or will do. To be loved for whom we are, accepted as we are with all our weaknesses and frailties: This is what we long for!

Rather than pointing to the beyond, families today tend to focus attention elsewhere. Pleasure, possessions, prestige, and power capture most minds and hearts. Race, identity politics, and secular ideologies follow close behind, as well as an abundance of trivial pursuits. In the end, all of these are futile ends which ultimately will fail to satisfy. We have lost our sense of belonging to whom we truly belong. Families are no longer the incubators of faith they once were. Rather than leading us to God, so many of them divert our attention away from him. Rather than pointing to the beyond, they point only to this-worldly pursuits. Rather than nurturing a sense of love and belonging, they succeed only in alienating us from one another and ultimately from God himself.

We need to look elsewhere. We need to rediscover our sense of the sacred and look beyond the here and now. We need to discover that our deepest yearning, our deepest need for belonging can only be filled by recognizing our need for God. St. Augustine put it best in his *Confessions*, "O Lord, we were made for Thee and our hearts are restless until they rest in Thee."[1] The message of Augustine and of the Lord he served is clear. We belong to God's family. We long for him. We belong to him. Much of our journey thorough life has to do with discovering this our deepest longing. We are all members of God's family. We are all returning home.

The Prodigal's Return

The parable of the prodigal son in Luke's

---

[1] Augustine of Hippo, *Confessions*, 1.1.

Gospel reminds us that we all belong in the home of the Father. It is a tale about God's unconditional love for his children. This love does not have any preconditions. The father in the story loves the younger son even when he asks for his share of the inheritance, squanders it on dissolute living, comes to his senses after losing everything, and returns home hoping to be treated as a mere servant. When he returns, his father does not merely accept him back, but runs out to meet him, dresses him in a fine robe, puts a ring on his finger, shoes on his feet, and orders his servants to prepare a feast. Similarly, when the elder son complains about the merciful treatment the younger son has received, the father reminds him of his love for him, assures him that everything he owns is also his, and says it was necessary to celebrate the prodigal son's return since he has finally come to his senses and returned home, "What was lost has been found." At the end of the parable, we never know if the elder son accepts his father's explanation and joins in the celebration of his younger brother's return.

Like the father in the parable, God loves us as we are. Whenever we wander away from him, he is always quietly waiting for us to "come to our senses" and return home where we belong. Whenever we are judgmental towards others and harbor resentment in our hearts, he is always quick to remind us of his love for us, encourages us to let go of our bitterness, share in his joy, and join in the celebration. Whatever our situation, whatever our difficulty, whatever our problem, whatever our sin, God is ever patient and merciful. He never forces his hand but is always waiting for us to look at the situation, be honest with ourselves, admit our mistakes, and return to him. If we make our way toward him, he will always rush out to meet us with open arms to welcome us home and celebrate our return.

There is probably a bit of the younger son and elder son in each of us. There are times when we decide to go our own way and refuse to stay in our Father's house. There are other times when we remain home, but somehow feel entitled to our status in life and become judgmental toward those who do not measure up to our standards of loyalty and faithfulness. In the midst of it all, the Father is quietly waiting for us. He is biding his time, waiting for us to open our eyes and see things under the light of his gentle grace. When we open our eyes and see things in the light of faith, we find new meaning in our present difficulties. Once we have the assurance of God's unconditional love for us, what was once deeply troubling to us suddenly dwindles in significance and becomes easier to bear. The reason why is because God's love can transform every human situation. It can bring order out of chaos, shed light in dark places, and heal broken bones, and make all things new. God's unconditional love for us reminds us that, wherever we are in our spiritual journey, we are all homeward bound and, in the words of St. Catherine of Siena, "All the way to heaven is heaven, because Jesus said 'I am the Way.'"[2]

Our Journey Home

Our spiritual journey leads us into the mystery of God. We can choose to enter into it, or we can choose to go our own way. The choice is ours to make. There is no turning back. At the end of the day, each of us has to decide. "Follow me" (Mt 4:19). Jesus' invitation is always there. We can choose to follow him, the path leading to life, or one of our own making, the path leading to death. We must choose to follow his way or go our own. If we choose the former, his Spirit will be there indwelling within us, inspiring us, and drawing us home.

These efforts, however, will not bear fruit, if we fail to listen to his voice. God speaks to us in

---

[2] Cited in Regis Martin, *The Last Things: Death, Judgment, Hell, Heaven* (San Francisco: Ignatius Press, 1998), 39; Kelly S. Johnson, *The Fear of Beggars: Stewardship and Poverty in Christian Ethics* (Grand Rapids, MI: Wm. B. Eerdmans Publishing Co., 2007), 209.

silence. His speaks in subtle tones, ones that lie deep beneath the clamor of noise that fills our daily lives. His words cannot be spoken, for they touch each heart in a way that is ineffable. The language of God is one of silence. If we wish to speak to him, we must first enter into the silence that surrounds us and seek to be still. If we learn to rest in this silence and be still, then God will speak to us. He will do so, however, not through words and images, but by means of a direct insight that can only be put into words only after it is tasted, savored, enjoyed, and reflected upon. God's Word is constantly drawing us home. His Spirit draws us through a grace-filled magnetic pull that leads us freely to himself, a self that enjoys the intimate love of the Father for his Son. Jesus is constantly searching for us and inviting us to follow him. We experience that pull throughout our lives. Sometimes it feels very strong; at other times, it appears to weaken and recede to the background. Whatever its intensity, it is always there, gently pointing us in the right direction and drawing us into the mystery of God.

Our spiritual journey is all about letting go and letting God. Jesus once referred to himself as the good shepherd whose sheep know his voice and follow it when they hear it. He is constantly speaking to us, calling each of us by name, and inviting us to come to him. His voice is quiet and still, one that be easily overlooked if we are not attentive. His voice speaks directly to our hearts. It comes to us not from the outside, but from within. To hear it, we must empty ourselves of all the clutter, noise, and busyness that fills our lives. Only when we are sufficiently free of life's many distractions, will we be able to hear his voice echoing down the canyons of our souls. Only then will we be able to discern the path that will lead us home.

Fullness of Life

We are able to find our way home only because God first found his way to us. We can go to God only because he first came to us. The good shepherd went out to find the lost sheep. What was lost has finally been found. The reason we can make our way to heaven is because God himself entered our world and became one of us to set us free from the slavery of sin and death. In becoming human, God brought heaven down to earth and lifted earth up into heaven, thus making a new heaven and a new earth. Our journey to God, therefore, was preceded by God's journey to us. He not only became man in the person of Jesus of Nazareth, but he is constantly seeking to dwell within our hearts and incorporate us into his body.

Jesus is the New Adam, the New Man. The term "Mystical Body of Christ" is not a mere poetry, but a complex divine-human reality with ramifications for us as individuals and as a community of believers. In Jesus, humanity has been transformed and lifted up to a higher realm of existence. Because of him, it is in the process of being divinized. That means that, at one and the same time, each of us is able to share in the divine nature, while also forming a part of a larger corporate personality. As believers, we are members of Jesus' glorified, risen body. His Spirit dwells within our hearts and enables us to share intimately in his life and consciousness. Because of him, we are also able to share in the intimate love of the Father for the Son and the Son for the Father. The gift of the Spirit is what binds us to Jesus, to the Father, and to one another. We can return to the Father only because Jesus has embraced our humanity, taken it into himself, transformed it, and lifted it to a higher realm.

Jesus, it is said, came to make all things new (Rev 21:5). Heaven for God was to take our broken humanity into himself, heal it, transform it, elevate it to new heights, and dwell within it. He calls us his friends and wants us to share in the mystery of divine love (Jn 15:15). In doing so, he allows us to dwell within his heart and he within ours. This mutual indwelling comes about by means of his Spirit, who enters our hearts, sanctifies us, and makes his abode there. Because of the Spirit, we are incorporated into Christ's transformed and glorified risen body. Because of the Spirit, we are Jesus' brothers and sisters and adopted sons and daughters of the Father. When the Father looks upon us, he sees his Son. We can approach the Father only through the Son. Any good we do is done through Jesus, with Jesus, and in Jesus, in the unity of the Holy Spirit. If it is true that the glory of God is man fully alive, it is only because Jesus himself underwent death so that we could share in the fullness of his life.

In My Father's House

What will we find at our journey's end? For centuries, people have tried to imagine what heaven will be like. We need only to read such works as Dante's *Divine Comedy*, Bunyan's *The Pilgrim's Progress* and, more recently, Lewis' *The Great Divorce* to get a small glimpse of the possibilities. The Book of Revelation offers this description of the Heavenly Jerusalem:

> And in the spirit, he [an angel] carried me away to a great, high mountain and showed me the holy city Jerusalem coming down out of heaven from God. It has the glory of

God and a radiance like a very rare jewel,
like jasper, clear as crystal. It has a great,
high wall with twelve gates, and at the
gates twelve angels, and on the gates are
inscribed the names of the twelve tribes of
the Israelites; on the east three gates, on
the north three gates, on the south three
gates, and on the west three gates. And the
wall of the city has twelve foundations, and
on them are the twelve names of the twelve
apostles of the Lamb.

(Rev 21:9-14)

The imagination, however, even the inspired
one, can only go so far. Regardless of how we
imagine heaven, we can rest assured that the reality will far exceed our meager attempts to describe
it. To be sure, the gap between the reality of
heaven and our imaginative depictions of it is
likely one of infinite proportions. In the end, it is
probably best that we simply place our trust in
Jesus' words to his disciples, "In my Father's
house there are many dwelling places. If it were
not so, would I have told you that I go to prepare
a place for you? And if I go and prepare a place for
you, I will come again and will take you to myself,
so that where I am, there you may be also" (Jn
14:2-3). Heaven is the place that Jesus is preparing for us. He has gone ahead of us to ready a

dwelling place especially suited to our needs and expectations.

The many dwelling places in our Father's house, may indicate that heaven may be perceived in a variety of ways, depending on our expectations, belief systems, and the way we lived our lives. The fact that they are all in the Father's house, however, indicates that each dwelling place will share a number of characteristics with the others.

To begin with, in heaven Jesus will draw us to himself and the bond will be so tight that it be impossible to break or become undone. Jesus is already readying us for this relationship by giving us the gift of his Spirit. The difference between now and then is that of the already-but-not-yet. Although Jesus is with is now through his Spirit, it is still possible for us to turn away from him and fall into sin. In heaven, we will be completely free and so totally immersed in his love that the very possibility of sinning would never enter our minds, let alone our hearts.

A dwelling place, moreover, is a place of rest. In heaven, we will be completely at rest. Our yearning and longing for God will be completely satisfied. Hope of reaching our destination will be turned into the enjoyment of having arrived and flourished there. In heaven our hunger and thirst for God will be fully satiated. Our souls will overflow with the light of divine grace and pour itself out into every dimension, every nook and cranny of our being. We will see God face to face, and God will smile upon the persons we have become.

Although heaven will transcend time and space as we know them, it will resemble them and, indeed, even transform them. Just as grapes mature and ferment into wine, so too time and space will themselves be transformed by God. In heaven, our resurrected bodies will have an aspect of materiality about them, but the matter comprising them will be transformed and glorified by the power of God. Rather than being bound by the present limitations of time and space, our resurrected and glorified bodies will transcend them. The "place" Jesus is preparing for us is not a "place" as we know it, but something so much more.

Although we will be completely at rest there, heaven will also hold out to us the possibility of continual adventure and discovery. Since God is infinite, there will always be something more for us to learn about him. Moreover, since we are made in his image and likeness, there will always be something more for us to learn about ourselves. Life in heaven will not be a static but a dynamic existence. Gregory of Nyssa (c. 335-c395) held that our spiritual journey will never end, since we will spend eternity immersing ourselves ever more deeply into the divine mysteries.[3]

In heaven we will experience the fullness of life. God's dream of who we are and what we could become will be a reality. Throughout our earthly sojourn God has been continually calling us home and drawing us through the inspirations of his Spirit into the intimacy of his divine friendship. This fullness of life gives glory and honor to God our Creator. It reveals the fullest scope of his creative, redemptive, and sanctifying power. God became human so that humanity might become divine. The fullness of life is to share in the very life of God himself and relish our identity as his adopted sons and daughters.

It is also important to remember that because God has given us free will it is possible that some may never choose to enter it. Hell is the absence of God, and some people choose to live in this shadowy void. C.S. Lewis once wrote that the gates of hell are locked from the inside. God wants everyone to live in his presence, but he refuses to force anyone against their will. Those who choose to go their own way are free to do so. The choice is theirs to make. God will not make it for them.

Finally, heaven is all about the vision of God (visio Dei). This involves not only God's vision of us, but also our vision of God. The latter, which is

---

[3] Gregory of Nyssa, *The Life of Moses*, 2.239.

also known as the beatific vision, represents the end of our spiritual journey. In this vision, the threefold way of purgation, illumination, and union will have run its course. We will see God face to face. What we experience, however, will depend in part on our capacity to receive him. We will be fully divinized, but each according to the place assigned to us in God's kingdom. The beatific vision, in other words, is not a homogeneous experience, but one full of variety. No two saints in heaven will experience God in exactly the same way.

Conclusion

Our journey through life is meant to be an initiation into the mystery of the divine. We are hardwired for God and, since God is love, we are also hardwired for love. Our spiritual journey has everything to do with our relationship with God. It is measured by our docility to his voice and our willingness to follow his commands. "I give you a new commandment, that you love one another. Just as I have loved you, you also should love one another" (Jn 13:34). Jesus demonstrated his love for us by entering our world, giving himself to us completely, to the point of dying for us, and by becoming nourishment for us and a source of hope. Those who follow him are called to do the same.

Our spiritual journey has everything to do with our relationship with Christ. He does not consider us his servants but his friends. He longs to dwell within our hearts and does so by the power of his Spirit. He invites us to follow him and promises to lead us to the house of his Father. He longs for us more than we long for him. Our journey towards him is but a faint reflection of his journey to us. He wants to live in our hearts and, if we are willing to follow the promptings of his Spirit, he invites us to live in his. He wants nothing more than to live in communion with us by allowing us to share in the intimacy of his divine life.

Our spiritual journey ends in the beatific vision when we will see God face to face. At that time, we will have passed through various periods of purgation and illumination and will have experienced various moments of union with God that lead to a deep existential experience of communion with the very ground of our being, the Creative Father, the Redeeming Son, and the Sanctifying Spirit, all of whom act as One and who vivify our lives by keeping us in being, healing us, and transforming us in such a way that we can enter into the presence of God. Our spiritual journey begins and ends in God. Our destination is God himself. Our way there is through Jesus Christ, our Lord, our Savior, our Redeemer, and our Friend. He who came to make all things new dwells within our hearts and promises to lead us through life, beyond death, into the house of his Father.

Returning Home

- We are all returning home. Where do you feel most at home? Is it when you are among family? Among friends? When you are alone? When you are at prayer? How do you feel when you go to church? Do you feel comfortable? Do you feel at home? Do feel you belong? Do you feel as though you belong to God?

- We are all wayward sons and daughters. With which character in the parable of the Prodigal Son do you identify with most? The wayward son? The elder brother? The father? Do you identify in some way with all three? How would you chart your journey home? What will it take for you to come to your senses?

- Returning home is all about letting go and letting God. What must you let go of in order to move forward? What unnecessary baggage are you carrying that is holding you back? Why are you holding on to these people and things? What would it take for

you to let go of them and trust God with
your safety and well-being?

- The glory of God is man fully alive? What
does "being fully alive" mean to you? Have
you ever felt that way? Have you ever felt as
though you were filled with the Spirit of the
Lord? How would you describe your
present state? Are you spiritually ill? Half
alive? Half dead? What could you do to
draw closer to God?

- What do you think heaven will be like? Do
any particular images come to mind? Do
you view it as a place? A state of mind? A
little bit of both? What do you think of the
saying, "Paradise for God is the human
heart?" What do you think of the saying,
"All the way to heaven is heaven?" what do
you think of the saying, "The kingdom of
Good is in your midst?"

Prayer

Lord, sometimes I feel as though I do not
belong anywhere. I long for you, but you seem
so distant and elusive. Help me not to succumb
to these feelings. At such times, help me to
walk by faith on my journey home. Help me
never to give up, but to always look for you in
the midst of difficult circumstances. I believe

in you Lord! I thirst for you! I long for you! Help my unbelief. Deepen in me the hope of one day seeing you face to face in the house of the Father. Although I can do nothing by myself, I believe that with you all things are possible.

Conclusion

As this book draws to a close, let us remember its one underlying premise: our spiritual journey begins and ends in God: We were created by him and for him; We were redeemed through him, with him, and in him; We are sanctified and made holy by the power of his Spirit. For some of us, this awareness of our redeemed and sanctified creaturely status comes rather easily and without many trials and hardships. For most of us, however, this discovery of our true identity as children of God requires a considerable amount of prayerful reflection. The spiritual journey is unique to each individual. Although our paths will cross at various points along the way, we tend to take very personal routes to our journey's end. In this sense, we are all wayward prodigals following a deeply personal, circuitous route on our journey home.

We travel together; we travel alone. Our purpose as God's children is to find our way to God and dwell in his heart. The more we search for God, however, the more we find that he too is searching for us and has already found us by entering our world and becoming one of us. God not only gave us a world to journey in, he also entered our world in the person of Jesus Christ to heal us of our self-inflicted wounds. Without him, we would never find our way home. Only he can to show us the way to the Father. He alone is "the way, and the truth, and the life" (Jn 14:6). As different as our journeys may be, they are all similar in that Jesus' redeeming love has made them possible. People of other faiths, even those who do not believe in him, are touched by his still voice—the voice of conscience—in the depths of their hearts. He speaks to the hearts of all men and women. God wants everyone to come to him. He wants everyone to return home. He wants everyone to experience the fullness of life. Those who listen to his voice and follow it will eventually do so because, in the end, they are merely responding to the promptings of his Spirit.

"The wind blows where it chooses" (Jn 3:8). As important as it was, God wanted to do more than simply enter our world and redeem it. He also wanted to enter our own personal worlds—your world and my world— so he could dwell there and live within us. He sent us his Spirit to do just that: to sanctify us and dwell within our hearts. The more we progress in our spiritual journey, the more we will get in touch with the promptings of the Spirit and his manifold gifts and fruits. The Spirit is the Paraclete, the Advocate, the Comforter. He wants to transform every aspect of our human makeup—the physical, emotional, intellectual, spiritual, and social— so that we can respond to his promptings, follow his lead, enter into the presence of God, and see him face to face. The best way to stay in touch with the promptings of the Spirit is to deepen our life of prayer.

Prayer is to our spiritual journey what air is in our earthly sojourn. We need to do it at all times. We need to take the words of the Apostle Paul to heart: "Rejoice always, *pray without ceasing*, give thanks in all circumstances; for this is the will of God in Christ Jesus for you" (1Th 5:17). Prayer is the great means of salvation. If we pray, we will eventually find our way home. If we do not pray, we will spend eternity trying to fill a giant hole in our soul that ultimately can only be filled by God. The choice is ours to make.

Since prayer is such an important part of our spiritual journey, it is fitting that we end this book with a guided meditation. What follows is a meditative prayer about our journey home. Read it slowly and reflectively. Allows the words to sink in and touch your heart. Allow them to lead you to that still point within your heart where the Spirit of God communes with your spirit, where heart speaks to heart, where you can lay bare your soul before the ground of our being, and simply rest in the surrounding silence. The poem that follows it, "The Traveler's Rest,"[1] suggests some helpful images for you to carry with you as you make you way home.

---

[1] Dennis J. Billy, "The Traveler's Rest," in *As There as the Sky* (Eugene, OR: Wipf and Stock, 2018), 16-17.

Our Spiritual Journey

A Guided Meditation

Each of us is on a journey.
We are traveling through life.
We travel together.
We travel alone.
No two journeys are alike.
Each one is different.
Some last but a few hours,
A few days,
Or years.
Others last a long time,
Or so it seems.
Seventy years,
Eighty years,
Ninety years—
In the Lord's eyes,
One day is like a thousand years,
And a thousand years are as a day.

Sometimes we feel close to our final destination.

Sometimes it seems far away.
Sometimes we feel like
We are wandering aimlessly about.
Moving forward,
But also moving away
From where we want to be,
From where we should be.
There is no turning back.
We are immersed in the Labyrinth of Life.
We are quietly being pulled
Toward the end of our journey.
We don't know how it will end,
Or where it will end,
Or when it will end,
Or even why it will end.
But it will end.
Make no mistake about it.
It will end.
And you will pass into nothingness.
For you are dust,
And unto dust you shall return.

Where did your earthly journey begin?
What are your earliest memories of it?
Are they happy ones?
Sad?
Painful?
What were your parents like?
Your family?

Did you feel loved?
Lonely?
Afraid?
What is your earliest memory of God?
What was he like?
Distant?
Harsh?
Judgmental?
Warm?
Loving?
Compassionate?

Look at Jesus as he journeys through life.
From the stable in Bethlehem,
To his workshop in Nazareth,
As he walked the roads of Galilee,
As he made his way to Jerusalem,
To the Temple Mount,
To the Upper Room,
To the Garden of Gethsemane,
To the Top of Golgotha.
His arms stretched out upon the cross,
Suffering,
Dying,
Breathing his last breath of air,
Commending his spirit
Into his Father's hands,
His body
Into his mother's arms.

Carried lifeless to the tomb,
To the darkness of death,
To the bowels of the earth,
To the depths of the Netherworld.

How will your journey end?
Where will you be?
Who will be with you?
Family?
Friends?
Will you be all alone?
Will Jesus be with you?
Will you have traveled with him?
Through good times?
Through bad times?
Were there times when
You felt estranged from him?
When you hid from him?
When you were tired?
When you were afraid?
When you felt lost?
When you lost hope?

Where was Jesus all this time?
Far away?
Quietly present?
Beside you?
In your heart?
Experiencing all you were experiencing?

Suffering with you?
Journeying with you?
Living and dying with you?
A fellow traveler?
A close, intimate friend?
Making you a part of himself?
Sharing in his Life after Life?
Making all things new?
Leading you home?
To his home?
To your home?
Into the mystery of God?
Into the depths of divine love?
Journeying with you?
Rising within you?
Within your heart?
Within his heart?

Will you allow him in?
Will you let him journey with you?
Will you talk to him?
Will you share your life with him?
Will you journey with him?
And allow him to lead you
Into the loving arms of his Father?
Talk to him in the quiet of your heart.
Even now, you and he
Are fellow travelers
On a never-ending journey.

The Traveler's Rest

Far have I come this day,
From there, beyond the ridge
As far as eye can see.
Every step, half taken,
Half left behind;
Every path not chosen—
Now lost in memory—
Brings my journey here.

Far have I come,
Through thicket and through fog,
Over mountain fastness,
In the mud and in the bog.
Far have I come—
A lonely traveler,
Foraging for rest
Beneath the restless sky.

Now my journey dwindles to a step,
As aching limbs and back,
Soreness of foot, each breath,

The pain of miles traveled,
And of miles yet to come,
The sweat—
All bid my bones
The peace of traveler's rest.

There, by the wayside,
My home will be this night—
With staff beside the fire
And head beneath the stars.
Silently the night will carry rest,
Until the darkness turns to dawn,
And the morning sun sheds its solitary light
Upon my chosen path.

Now, at this quiet hour,
When shadows cast no more
And darkness covers day,
I remember moments passing
And think of moments yet to come—
Moments which speak of my journey,
Which dwindle to a breath
And bring my weariness rest.

Heavy the lid falls upon the eye,
As the mind returns to dreaming,
As the soul becomes the sky.
Asleep in sleep, I wander
Through a thousand journeys,

To a thousand wayside places,
To a thousand unknown destinations—
And a single rude awakening.

Life is a journey, as is death—
And man, the traveler.
His every breath, a step;
His every step, the breath of a journey ended:
Night dwindles into dawn,
The day into dusk,
The journey into the traveler's rest,
The traveler into his final hour.

www.ingramcontent.com/pod-product-compliance
Lightning Source LLC
La Vergne TN
LVHW011359080426
835511LV00005B/341